T0157400

A Road
without a Map

Rose Aimée

iUniverse, Inc.
Bloomington

A Road without a Map

iUniverse books may be ordered through booksellers or by contacting:

iUniverse
1663 Liberty Drive
Bloomington, IN 47403
www.iuniverse.com
1-800-Authors (1-800-288-4677)

ISBN: 978-1-4620-5610-1 (sc)
ISBN: 978-1-4620-5611-8 (hc)
ISBN: 978-1-4620-5612-5 (e)

Library of Congress Control Number: 2011917188

Printed in the United States of America

iUniverse rev. date: 10/31/2011

Contents

೫◊೩

Dedication

To my children and grandchildren:
You are my pride and joy,
I hope you all enjoy reading my story.
I proudly want to tell you,
"You inspired me to write this book."
I have recorded my memories.
I have wanted to share them with you for a long time.
To Angela and Eric,
"Thank you for your help."
To my husband, James,
"Thank you for your encouragement
and your understanding."
To Connie and Ann,
"Thank you for all your help.
I could not have done it without you."

Introduction

❧❦❧

Named Rose Aimée, I was born in a remote part of Quebec in 1938. Life was hard. At a young age, I begged my father to move us closer to the rest of our family, who lived in a village twelve miles away. Living where I did was a type of exile, at least in my eyes. Early in my teen years, I looked for work, found a job, and left home just to feel the freedom of being able to live on my own. I still can't comprehend why I had to struggle so long and so hard to survive for so many years. I fell many times but always managed to get up. My pride had more scrapes than my knees!

My first memoir, *Wander*, recalls the winter of 1943, when I was five years old. My family lived in a cabin in the Quebec woods, and we suffered through one of the worst winters of our lives. This memoir recounts the memories I have from that time until 2010. Many of the memories contain painful secrets; others are filled with happiness.

Chapter 1

Starting School

❦

In 1945, at the age of seven and a half, I started school in a one-room schoolhouse in the remote area of Quebec where I lived.

It was the beginning of August. My sister Gisele and I were picking blueberries out in the field. Our buckets were finally full of those small berries, and we were exhausted by the heat and labor it took to get the chore done. I wouldn't dare go back home before my bucket was full. I was too proud; I had to finish the job. I was the older sister, and I had to set a good example for Gisele. On our way home, we stopped at a small creek to drink water. There was an empty aluminum can left there for people to use if they needed water as they passed by.

When we got home, there was a car in the driveway. It belonged to Robert, the only person we knew in our area who owned a car. Robert was an associate with the school system and had the respect of the community. I knew that his visit had to be important. When Gisele and I went in the house, we were welcomed with big smiles. This made me apprehensive, as the looks were directed especially at me. Robert had told my parents that they needed to send me to school because they needed a certain number of students to

1

open the school. He asked me some questions. I was a bit scared and didn't understand what the fuss was about. If the school had enough students without me, I would not have to attend. However, I never would have had the ability to write about my experience today. After a long discussion between Robert and my parents, they agreed that I would be starting school in a few days.

The school was only a mile from my house, not a long distance away, but for me, a young child it may as well have been the other end of the world. The only road available stretched a quarter of a mile through the woods. That road was bordered by forest on both sides, where I knew that wild animals often roamed, so I was terrified. I liked those animals from afar, but meeting one face-to-face on the road would be a different story. That is why school had been out of my reach until then. Walking alone on that road was too risky.

On the first day of school, my father came with me through the woods, carrying a sporting gun, until I could see our neighbor's house. He went with me every day until winter began. At that point, I was fine. I always walked home alone. I had become used to the look of the dark forest. In the spring, there were mama bears protecting their cubs. I was lucky for a long time and never encountered anything but wild rabbits and deer.

One day the next fall, coming back home and singing as loudly as I could, I saw a large bear eating leaves from a tree on the side of the road. I had been told that it is much less likely to see those types of wild animals because they will run away if they hear noise. All that singing didn't do me any good. I could not take the chance of going by that beast. To the left of the road was a large open space, so I decided to take a detour. My legs were shaking, but I ran as fast as I could. The bear didn't seem to be bothered by me and continued to eat. I was never so scared in my life. It took some of the fun away from going to school. Finally my sister Gisele was old enough to start school; my fear was gone, because there were two of us going together through the woods. I had two other siblings at home Louiselle and Jacques, but they were too young for school.

My first teacher was Miss Janette. She had been teaching for two years. I will never forget how she made me feel. She was a gentle woman, always full of concern for every student. She had shoulder-length brown hair that was always well combed, and she was beautiful in every sense of the word. She was my idol, someone I wanted to be like when I grew up. I learned more from her in two years than in all the rest of my school years combined.

My first day of school was an event I will never forget. I was given a notebook and a pencil, the most precious tools I had ever received. The first few years I went to school were such a revelation to me. I never knew much about the outside world. I was shy. I had never been exposed to strangers, and I lived in a different world. Miss Janette was extremely patient with me and took the time to explain all that was expected of me, and I made sure she would not be disappointed. Because of my teacher's patience, I was willing to learn. She knew how to make me proud of all my accomplishments, and I strived to make the most of the several months I was in school each year. I was learning, so everything was new. I felt inferior to the other students, because of my size even though I was older. They were more advanced. I was ashamed of how little I knew, but I finally got better at catching up to the other students. I was so proud of myself after every small accomplishment. Miss Janette taught me not to give up. I will never forget her; I have to thank her for many things. I only have good memories of my first two years at school.

In our school, there was a library with about one hundred books. I read every one of them, and some I read many times. If I liked the story, I would ask my teacher if I could keep the book longer than allowed. She would allow me a few extra days. I was so happy to find one story called "*The Child Lost and Found*". In French, its title is "*L'Enfant Perdue et Retrouvè*". My mother told us that story many times when we were small children. It was about a family that had too many children, so they decided to "lose" one of their boys in the forest. The story was about all the misery and adventures that child had until he found his way home; by then, he was in his twenties. That story was every child's nightmare, especially those in large families.

The third year, all the good things about school changed when we got another teacher, one without any experience. Miss Julie was nothing like Miss Janette. She was self-centered, and all the students were on edge because of her temper and got a round of ruler hitting on the palms of their hands for one reason or another. I escaped the hitting, but Miss Julie was always looking for ways to belittle me. From the way she talked to me, I could feel that she didn't like me. Her large breasts were always in my face. I remember having the multiplication table of three to learn, but I hadn't had time to study, so I didn't know the answer. I tried to explain that I didn't have the time to study since my mother was sick and I had to make dinner, clean up the younger children, and put them to bed. After a long day at school and the work that I had to do at home it was time for me to go to bed. I was so tired that I forgot that I had to memorize the table of threes. It was to no avail that I tried to explain. The teacher humiliated me in front of the entire class. She told me to stay in front of the class on my knees and study the table of threes until I knew it by heart. She added that I should wash my clothes because I was dirty. So I stayed on my knees most of the day just to defy her and let her know I would learn when I was ready. Until that day, I'd never had a reprimand from my teacher. I was so humiliated that I never learned the multiplication table of three until thirty years later, when I needed to do some math for accounting in my business. This humiliation taught me that childhood experiences are very important.

In December 1946, I had another of my first steps in growing up, an event for which my mother and my teacher had prepared me. My father took me to the midnight Mass on Christmas Eve, and I received my first Holy Communion. My mother had made me a new dress for that special event. She didn't have enough fabric for the entire dress, so the skirt was navy blue, and the top was a lighter blue, with white rickrack around the collar and the sleeves.

Before receiving First Holy Communion, each child had to go to confession for the first time. At eight, I already had a long list of sins, all venial, but I was scared of what the priest would impose as a penance for forgiveness of those bad things I had done. I was surprised and relieved when he gave me a penance to say a few "Ave Maria's", but I returned to the bench with my head hanging down because I felt as if everyone knew what I had just confessed.

I went to school only in the fall and spring, not the winter months, so I missed at least two months a year. This made it hard for me to keep up with the program. I went up a grade every year, and when I was twelve, I was supposed to go to grade five when we graduated from our classes in the spring. The last two years had been hard for me; my mother had been sick all the time with some kind of depression. As the oldest of five children, I was responsible for everything in the house, including cooking and washing. My younger brother was crying all the time. So instead of moving to fifth grade when I was twelve, I stopped going to school after my parents discussed it and agreed that home would be the best place for me.

They also agreed that in two years, after my younger sister Gisele and two other younger siblings could take over, I would go to a special school where I could learn how to sew and become a seamstress. Since I loved the latest fashions, this six-month training would be helpful. However, it never happened. Instead, I continued helping my father on the farm and my mother in the house. I missed going to school. Every morning I would look at the children walking to the place where I wanted to be, but I had no choice. I was the oldest child and a girl, so I didn't need much instruction. At least, that is what they said in those days.

I did love to sew. I had received an old Singer sewing machine from my maternal grandmother. I had made some money babysitting the neighbor's children, and bought some fabric to make two dresses, one for Gisele, and one for me. They would be our Christmas dresses. I got some black taffeta fabric, a small piece of red corduroy, and a few rhinestones, and I made Gisele's dress first. The skirt and half of the top were black. The rest of the top was a scalloped red corduroy yoke, with a rhinestone on each scallop. As soon as I finished Gisele's dress, I started on mine. I quickly realized that I was short on fabric, so I made my skirt a bit too tight. As a result, I had to take short steps every time I walked while wearing that dress during the Christmas season. I was so proud of myself; at thirteen, I knew nobody could create a better masterpiece.

Later that winter, a woman came to the village for a week to teach sewing. After some begging, I got my parents to agree to send me to those classes. I was delirious with joy. I stayed for free with a friend of my father's in the village that week while I took the classes. I just had to help at their restaurant to pay for room and board. The classes cost $3.50 for the whole week, payable at the end of the day on Friday, when my father was supposed to pick me up.

The class finished at 3 p.m., but my father did not come for me. I waited and waited. I was embarrassed, as everyone was leaving and I didn't know what to do. The teacher asked me where my father was, and I did not have an answer. My face was red with shame. As it was starting to get dark, a friend of the teacher came to my rescue. She agreed to loan me the money to pay for the class if I promised to have my father repay her.

I left the place and walked to where I had been staying for

the week. My father was there waiting for me, but without the money. How bad I felt is hard to describe, but he promised me that he would pay the woman for the loan the next week. The next time he went to the village, he had to pass by the woman's house. I reminded him about the money, and when he came home he assured me that he had paid her. A few months later I received a note from the woman asking me to "Please repay the loan." I was lucky to have saved some money from babysitting jobs and I used this money to repay her. This was another reminder that I only had myself to count on. I just had to wish and hope that independence would come.

I was always aware that my lack of education caused difficulties in my life. I was forever reading everything I could put my hands on to try to educate myself. I never was a fiction buff; my reading was all about learning something new. Later in life my reading and learning came in handy. When I made a new friend, I never let on that I had only finished fourth grade. All my friends thought I had been in school much longer. When I was in a high position in a company, I always managed to fit in. I never talked about my past. It was my secret.

Chapter 2

The World of Work

⁂

My First Business

During November 1948, when I was ten years old, times were hard. I wanted to make some money for food and for Christmas gifts for my family. I was small for my age, but nothing was going to scare me. I had my mother order some Christmas cards from a sales ad in the newspaper. I didn't have any choice but to try selling those cards, and with the money I made, my mother could get food for the family. I was also a bit adventurous and wanted to try new things. I don't remember how many of those cards I had to sell, but I had to do something about our situation. I had many other ideas for making money, but my parents would not let me do anything, especially my mother. She was always afraid that something would happen to me. I had many arguments with her on that subject.

I knew how to harness the horse and attach it to the sled. I had watched and practiced under my father's supervision. Since I was short, I took the horse close to the porch and dragged the harness onto it. It wasn't easy, especially when my mother was around, because I felt anxious with her watching and worrying. She was

9

always warning me when she came out to check the harness to make sure it was attached safely. After getting in the sled I said, "Getdiup", and started on my way.

It was a sunny day right after lunch, a good time to start out selling my cards, even though there was snow on the road. I wore warm clothes. At my first house, I was lucky; the woman bought a few cards and gave me seventy-five cents. At that moment I knew I was born to sell, and I kept on going. I completely forgot about the time and did not turn back until I had sold all my cards. My mother had told me not to go too far. "Turn back at the fork," she had warned, but I completely forgot about the warning and went on until I was all out of merchandise.

There was a grocery store on the way back home, so I decided to get some food for the family. It was during the war, the time of rations, and each family was only allowed so much sugar every month. I am not sure how I did it, but I got sugar without the stamps I was supposed to have. Maybe the owner felt sorry for me. I got home when it was dark, and my mother was worried to death about me. But I was the happiest child in the world, and I was proud of myself. It was a while before I could go back on the road again — you can imagine why!

I was about fifteen years old when my sisters Louiselle and Gisele took over my work at home and I started to work at a long stream of places. By that time, I knew that I had been brought up in a primitive way. I'd learned so much in such a short time, and if I wanted to evolve, I would have to learn a lot more. First I would have to learn how to speak French correctly. I didn't know how to speak in my own language very well. My French was slangy most of the time, and I did not realize that I was speaking the farmer's tongue.

After I stopped going to school, I read everything I could get my hands on. I used to read *"Roman Feuilleton"* by the window in the moonlight in our small bedroom. It was a section written in a weekly newspaper. I was so interested in the story, but it was continued every week. I had to wait for my father to go to the store the next week and bring the next part of the story. If I was lucky, maybe he would bring me the end, maybe the final chapter. Lucky for me, he did!

I wanted to know what was going on in the rest of the world, but everything was a mystery and new to me. I kept reading voraciously. I was amazed at the ways of the world around me.

Cabano

I started my first job in the early spring of 1953, working as a housekeeper for an old woman who lived in Cabano, which was near my hometown, Saint-Eusèbe. She had an invalid husband who required a lot of attention. Their son was also living with them. I could not go in her quarters or in the husband's room. The shades were closed, and all I could see was the darkness when they entered and left the room. Even on a sunny day, I could see only the darkness. I always wondered what was going on in that room. I mostly worked in the kitchen, where I prepared some of the meals. The woman would come in the kitchen and get her husband's food, returning the empty dishes after the meal. Except when she was going in or out of the room, the door was kept closed at all times. That room was a scary place.

I also washed clothes, ironed, and did any other chores that needed to be done to keep the house clean. The kitchen was in the back of the house, so I didn't see anything that was going on in the front of the house. I had a bedroom upstairs, where I went after I finished my work. It faced the backyard, and that was all I could see. I never set foot in any other room in that house, except the hallway, from where I could see elaborate things. The furniture was massive, and the curtains were made with thick embroidered fabric. This was such a boring place to work that I decided I should look for another job.

When I was in the kitchen working, the old woman would sneak upstairs. I would hear the floor above creaking in the room that was mine. I am not sure what she was expecting to find. The only thing there was a pile of old magazines that kept me company during those long evenings when I was alone.

Every day around noon, the son who worked at the post office came to help his mother give some kind of hot or cold bath to the father. I never saw this happen, but I sure remember the father screaming in pain every time they gave him his treatment. I always thought they were torturing him. It upset me, and I didn't trust them. This was the first time I was out on my own. Communication with my parents was by letters only, as they did not have a telephone. I wrote to them about the situation, and soon after, my father and his friend Paul came to get me. It was short notice, but I quickly got in the pickup truck; I had been there for about two months.

Saint-Eusèbe

In the summer of 1953 I left Cabano and went back to my village of Saint-Eusèbe to work in a small hotel, similar to a boardinghouse. I can't remember the name of it, but Mr. Paul Dubois owned it. It was hard work, and the stress was high. Mr. Dubois had a son, Raymond, by his first wife, and when she died, he had married a younger woman a few years later. Mr. Dubois had a furious temper that kept everyone on edge. He didn't treat his wife very well, and she seemed to be afraid of her husband. At any moment, he would burst in a rage for no reason. His wife was the object of this rage and took most of the abuse without any complaining. She told me that she was pregnant and too scared to tell him.

To my amazement, a few days later, she told me that he was happy about the baby. I remember her beautiful smile. She was a pretty woman, and he should have been proud of her. She had lots of talent and was working hard as an all-around hotel owner's wife. Everyone knew how he treated her and anyone else close to him, but no one seemed to think that treatment was abuse, and they turned their backs on her. No one interfered, as they were husband and wife. A wife never complained about her husband. It was a barrier that could not be breached.

Mr. Dubois also abused his son, even though he wasn't doing anything bad. I remember the day he wanted seven-year-old Raymond to use the horse to pull something out of the ground, but the horse kept on kicking. His son was scared. His father started to beat him up, and then threw him into a hole. People watched but were too scared to do anything until a neighbor came to his rescue. I thought the father was going to kill the son for sure.

Another time he threw his son into the cellar through a trap door that was in the kitchen floor. There was no light down there, and the child begged him to open the door. I was not supposed to open the trap door, but I kept watch, and when no one was home, I gave him some food, but I was too scared to truly help him. I do not remember how long the son was in the cellar, but eventually he was rescued. Mr. Dubois seemed to hate Raymond. I believe that he blamed him for the death of his first wife since she had died giving birth to his son.

I had been working for Mr. Dubois in the hotel for a few weeks and missed my family, even though they were only three miles away. A neighbor's brother offered to take me home to visit because he said that he had to talk to my father. The ride would not take long so I jumped at the offer because I had been good friends with his nieces, who were about my age, and I felt it was safe to go with their uncle. I told Mrs. Dubois that I was going to visit my family for a couple of hours.

Halfway to the house, the man pulled over. He looked at me in a strange way and did not say anything. When he parked the car, I asked what was going on. In an instant, he was on top of me, trying to pull off my clothes. I was taken by surprise; I didn't know what was going on. I defended myself the best I could. I was petrified, but screaming wasn't an option since we were much too far from any house.

Suddenly, a truck came, and the two men in it didn't waste any time coming to my rescue. They took me to their truck. One of the men was my boss, Mr. Dubois, who had found out from his wife that I was on my way home with this guy. He held down my attacker, and the other guy gave him a few punches. I did not go home; instead, they drove me back to my workplace.

I was lucky that time. God must have loved me. I learned later that the man had just been released from a mental hospital. He had committed rape before, but instead of jail, he had been confined to that hospital. No one ever talked about things like that in my time. Rape happened, but it was always a family secret. For a long time after, I was afraid of men and hated them. I never talked about the incident to anybody. It was my way of coping with it.

Mr. Dubois never treated me as he treated his wife and son, but I didn't like to see all that violence around me. So another time when I was visiting my parents, I told them about the problem and decided to quit. It was such a relief to be out of that house after the summer ended.

I forgot about Mr. Dubois. Later, when my father met him, he had a small business selling arts and crafts. He talked to my father about how he had changed. He said that he was now a man of God and had converted to a cult. He could perform miracles when asked to do so. When my father told me this about Mr. Dubois, I knew that he was a dangerous man.

Edmunston

I had not been back to Saint-Eusèbe long when I went to work in Edmunston, a city in New Brunswick. Soon after my return home after my summer job at the hotel, two men had stopped at our house and told my mother that someone in the village had told them that I was looking for a job. I wasn't, but I was available. No one knew anything about those two men, but my mother made the decision for me to go to work for them.

I packed some clothes, got in the pickup truck, and sat on the front seat between the two of them. I was petrified. They drove for what seemed like an eternity to me. When we reached the town, we went to the house where I would be working. An older woman opened the door. She was smiling, and I thought she was pleasant, but she seemed surprised that I was to stay with her. She showed me to a room that was extremely clean. The whole house shone. I had been told that she needed a cleaning woman. I thought it was strange because the woman looked capable of doing her tasks. I helped her do the dishes; then she told me that was all I had to do for that day and to go to my room to rest.

Thinking the woman was a bit different, it didn't take me long to realize that she had a problem, a big one. She had some kind of mental illness, maybe dementia, which was all strange to me. I did not know anyone with that kind of sickness. I used to lock my bedroom door and put things in front of the door so if she tried to enter, the noise would awaken me. She had told me that the Virgin Mary was visiting my room at night.

One day when the men had gone to work, she decided to take me into the basement. She told me not to tell the men we had gone there. She showed me some kind of big machinery and said that she didn't know what was going on. She thought it was some kind of invention her son was working on. I could not tell what that machine was used for, but I also thought that it was some kind of invention the son was trying to put together. After all, he was only seventeen at the time.

The father and son went into the basement every day, working on this machine. The son was big and tall; he was a part-time worker for a radio station, broadcasting play-by-play for wrestling matches every Saturday night. The son and his father actually took me to a match one time. At the intermission, someone sang.

The only people I saw every day were those three people; they were good to me. The work was light, so most of the time we watched TV or read. The woman acted normal most of the time, but was also a bit unpredictable. Sometimes I would go for a walk with her, but I was told not to go too far. I am not sure why I left this job, but I know that it had taken me away from my family. For the first time I missed my siblings but I was happy to contribute some income to my family.

My next job was back in Saint-Eusèbe. I worked as a housekeeper for a family with five boys, ranging in age from two to nine. The mother was a school teacher. She left early in the morning and was back for dinner. Her husband took care of the farm animals. There was a lot of work to do: washing, cleaning house, mending clothes, and cooking. I did not even know how to make a bed properly, but I knew how to sew. The mother had been informed that I liked to sew. My first assignment was to make shirts for the five boys out of dark blue checkered cloth. There was no way to rest at any time during the day. I worked from six in the morning until nine at night. The five boys and their parents kept me busy, but I enjoyed working for this nice family. They treated me like a daughter.

The husband liked to party. Every weekend he and his wife were invited to some kind of celebration, and I was included. I looked forward to having fun, and the weekends always had some excitement for me. An invitation to a dance did make up for a week of hard work. At seventeen, I was small for my age and sometimes got looks that I did not like. I acted my age but looked more like I was thirteen. Being innocent was a blessing; I felt different, but not guilty for looking young. I did make friends. One special friend, Aline, was my good friend for many years.

My first experience with interest from the opposite sex made me feel almost normal. I was introduced to a friend of my boss, an army boy named Roger. I was delighted; for me, it was my first "love" adventure. I was sure he would get tired of me soon, but for the time we had, we laughed and we danced. He wrote me a few letters, and I wrote back to him. I lived for those words of friendship. It would take me so long to read those letters. His handwriting was hard to understand, but that didn't matter to me. I was just so happy to get a letter from him.

Most of the boys did not go to school for more than three or four years. Roger was the exception. He was in the army and learning a trade at the same time the war was going on. Maybe someday he would be a war hero. Our friendship lasted for a while until he was sent away on some mission and my job also finished with the family when school ended for the year. Roger and I wrote to each other a few times, but finally the flame was extinguished. Both of us went in new directions, but I often thought about him.

These jobs were my first encounters with the real world. What a big lesson for me. There was so much to learn, including that there was a new world so close to me but so far away at the same time.

Rivière-Bleu

In the spring of 1957, when I was nineteen, I went to work at a small restaurant called Laney in Rivière-Bleu, a small town about twenty miles from my parents' home. The owners were kind people, almost like parents to me. The wife was very clean and insisted that our uniforms, black skirts and white long-sleeved blouses, be pressed and starched. It was fun to be neat and well groomed. I made many friends at that restaurant. It was a *rendez-vous* for everyone in the town, but mostly for young people like me. Two of the girls, Aline and Rachel who worked with me, became like sisters to me. We were inseparable. Aline was the pretty one and the more ladylike of the three of us. Rachel was the willing one. I was the instigator and the planner. Rachel would follow, and Aline was always putting the brakes on many of my pranks. I never did anything to get us in trouble; I just enjoyed a good laugh. I haven't changed much. I still laugh a lot!

I was never satisfied when life was always the same. I wanted adventure, to try something new. In September of that year, Aline decided that we should go to Bangor, Maine to pick potatoes because we could make lots of money in a short time. I quit my restaurant job, and Aline, my cousin, Lacasse, a few friends, and I drove to Bangor. The job lasted about five weeks. Many mornings there was frost on the ground. It was dirty, cold, and the food was awful. It was the hardest work I had ever done. I was short and weighed about ninety pounds, and the bucketfuls of potatoes weighed about the same as me. After a few hours of picking, we had to drag those buckets up to the big barrel so the truck could pick them up and bring them to a large container, something like a train car. It was almost impossible to lift those buckets into the big barrel, and we had to keep up. Because I was a girl, sometimes the boys helped me lift those buckets. I was the lucky one. Many of the girls could not keep up. By the end of the day, we were all exhausted. The trucks made the rounds, picking up the full barrels.

We lived in some kind of empty camp that had a room where two of us girls slept. The boss and his wife lived in the main house. The kitchen was equipped with a woodstove for cooking and a large table with a bench on each side. On Sundays, we had the day off. We needed to rest.

One Sunday we decided to go to St. Pascal, Maine, which was the nearest town. It had a roller skating rink. I had never tried to skate before, but I was always willing to try something new. One of my friends decided to teach me how to skate. I started out fine, but when he thought I was ready to skate alone, he let go of my hand. I fell on my back on the floor, taking him down on top of me. The other skaters were going around us at a hundred miles an hour. I finally got back up on my feet and went back to the bench. I didn't try to skate again for the rest of the night, but I had many laughs about that night.

The next morning for breakfast the cook made fresh doughnuts. My friends and I looked at each other and said, "Oh, no. Not roller skate wheels!" We called doughnuts "skate wheels" thereafter. I didn't make much money picking potatoes, but I enjoyed being with people my age. However, I would never do this job again.

In November 1957, I returned to Rivière-Bleu and resumed my job at Laney's restaurant. One day a customer came in to buy cigarettes. This was unusual, but I recognized the customer as the young man that I had worked for in Edmonston three years ago, taking care of his mother. When I asked about her, he seemed agitated. He had given me a twenty-dollar bill, and suddenly he decided not to buy the cigarettes. I gave him his money back, and we said good-bye. A few days later, the police came to the restaurant, showed us a photo, and asked if we had seen that person. I remembered seeing him and recounted the incident that had happened a few days earlier. I also told the police officer that I had his address in my address book. This is when I realized that the "invention" in the basement of their home in Edmunston was a money-printing machine. This was why no one was allowed to go down into the basement. They had been printing money for a while and had gotten away with it, probably because the lady of the house had some mental problems. You never know when you will see someone from the past. After all, the world is small.

In Rivière-Bleu, in the spring of 1958, I met Jean-Paul, my first real boyfriend. He was the older son of the town's mayor, and his parents apparently were well-to-do in the town. His father also owned a grocery store and a garage where they repaired trucks and sold cars. There were many other businesses in the town. The family home was located across the street by the river. On Sundays, Jean-Paul would often take me to his parents' home for dinner. The home included a cluster of rental buildings and a small, well-furnished chalet. One Sunday his mother took me inside the chalet. According to her, the chalet would be a starting house for their son and his future wife. There were brand-new appliances, including a toaster, in a teal blue color. The house was nice, definitely adequate for a small family, but to this day, the teal blue color still sticks in my mind. Looking at the house made me think twice about my relationship with Jean-Paul. I was flattered by all the attention I was getting from him and especially from his mother, but I realized I would be their daughter-in-law more than the wife of their son.

One summer night, I helped my boss deliver food late in the evening to a customer I had known for some time. When we went in the house, I found not only this customer but also Jean-Paul sitting on the couch being cozy. It shocked me, and I was hurt thinking that I had been deceived in this manner. Probably for a while, it was my pride that was hurt the most. His friend "the customer" was a phone operator and was able to listen to all my conversations, an amazing situation. I stopped making phone calls to anyone. Then a friend and I made up some kind of code so people couldn't understand what we were saying when they eavesdropped on us. It was lots of fun using our jargon to talk on the phone. I continued to see Jean-Paul for a few months after that episode, but our relationship wasn't very pleasant. All trust was gone.

There wasn't much to do in the town besides go to movies and visit friends' houses to listen to music, so we often ended up at his parents' house for dinner as well as on small occasions. We could also watch TV, a luxury in those years. I thought I was in love but later realized that what I loved was all the attention I was getting from Jean-Paul and his family. I also realized that the mother was the one in love with me. Eventually, everything went flat between Jean-Paul and me, and we stopped seeing each other. It didn't take long for me to get back to my regular life. By then, I had friends and I still was enjoying my freedom.

One year later, I left the restaurant for good and went to work for the Ouillette family at their general store in the same town, Rivière-Bleu. The store had a post office and sold all kinds of merchandise, like all general stores of that time. I had been there for over a year when a fire started on the day before Easter behind the house where I was staying. It burned everything: one private house, a restaurant, the large home, and the store where I was working. My bedroom was the first part of the house to burn. Everything I had was gone, including the few things I had acquired with my hard-earned money. I barely had anything left to wear.

We all took refuge with a neighbor for the night. The family and I had to live in another rented house for part of the year while the rebuilding was going on. It was a most humiliating time. The owner had received money from the insurance company but never gave me a cent to replace some of the things that I had lost, even though he had the money to do it. I continued to work for the family that year, cooking, washing, and cleaning all day long. I was very attached to the five children and loved each one of them almost like a big sister. I also made good friends, but the money was not enough for me to continue working there. When I thought about those days, I swore I would never be cheap like that boss.

Quebec

After the fire, I decided to move to Quebec City, where I hoped to find a better-paying job. It was now the summer of 1960. Through a friend, I found a position in a motel called Captain's Motel. I was hired over the phone, and when I arrived there, I met the two other workers who were the boss's daughters. After a week, I noticed that several of the customers were renting rooms mostly by the hour. I quickly figured out what was going on in those motel rooms, and I stayed away from the renting office. Every week I had to beg for my pay. One day near the end of the season, I was talking with a restaurant worker from across the street. He told me that my boss never paid his employees on a regular basis. The next day when I asked for my pay, he told me that I would have to wait for it until the season ended.

I called a restaurant, the Horizon, looking for a job, and they hired me over the phone that very day. Luckily, I had saved a few dollars, enough to pay for a taxi, for my room for one week, and for a few cookies for the next day. Meals were included in my job. With the tips I would be okay. The next day at my new job, I called the labor department and told them my story. That night, two big police officers met me after work at the place where I was now staying. They told me that since the motel owner was an ex-wrestler and a huge man, he had been using his size to scare previous employees, and he was doing the same to scare me. I got my pay and a little extra. I finally was defending myself, another big step toward independence.

Rivière-du-Loup

During that summer, a person who knew me from Rivière-Bleue and who had bought a hotel in Riviere-du-Loup asked me to work for him. So I left the Horizon right away and moved to Rivière-du-Loup to start yet another job. I also got a second job in a diner just for the summer. Wow, was I busy with these jobs, working at the diner by day and at the hotel by night.

Rivière-du-Loup was a small city by the lower Saint Lawrence River. In the summer it was very busy with tourists mostly from Montreal and Toronto. I was working long hours for low wages; surely there was no future for me there. I was not interested in getting married; at least I didn't think there was anyone of interest to me. So I made another decision to move on with my life.

For most of my young life, I worked in restaurants or hotels, which meant that I did not have weekends off. When everyone else was relaxing, it was time for me to work long, hard hours, entertaining the rest of the world. At the time, it did not seem fair. I was young and enjoyed fun things just like my friends, especially when there was some kind of event going on.

By the end of my teenage years the start of a real me emerged, a person with courage to fight for myself and believe in me. What a ride I had from the valley to the top of the mountain and back down to the ravine on my way to the top again. Sometimes I had been so far down that I never thought I would reach the top again. These experiences made me eager to discover new ways to a better life. I was never scared to work hard, and there wasn't much I could not do. I could fake it if I had to, and most of the time I succeeded. Defeats and triumphs taught me how to survive. I realized that destiny was in charge of my life, no matter how much I planned. Destiny would always take me on the road it had traced for me.

I now realize that I was searching for a better life in the wrong places, and my patience had become extremely limited. I was always anxiously looking for something, but I didn't know for sure what it was that I sought. That confusion brought me much heartache yet led me to many adventures.

Chapter 3

My Daughter Martine

彩

Martine's story begins in Rivière-du-Loup, where, in the spring of 1960, I was working a summer job as a server in a small coffee shop. One morning a handsome man came into the shop and asked for a cup of coffee. He introduced himself as Danny and started talking with me. He seemed like a charmer. When he left, I forgot about him, but he came back later that afternoon and asked me out for dinner. My workday was over and I was closing the place, but since he was so polite, I accepted his invitation. I was working two jobs and didn't have much time for entertainment. It sounded good to have some time out since those kinds of occasions were limited for me. From then on, he called me often, telling me that he was in town. He asked if I would accompany him to some outings, and if I had time off, I gladly accepted. We had some good times, and until the fall, our relationship was casual. When my summer job ended at the end of September, things got more serious. Since I was now working only one job, I had more time to see him.

Later that fall, I decided to move to Montreal to be with my friend Aline and her husband, Carto. Aline had told me that she was lonely and wanted me to get a job there so we could do things together. I liked Aline and Carto; we had been friends for a while, and like sisters and brothers, we took care of each other. I lived with them in Montreal for a while. I found a job right away in a department store similar to Macy's. I worked in the women's clothing section and loved my job. Over the years, I lost track of both of Aline and Carto; they moved, and I moved too much for them to keep up with me. Aline was a beautiful girl. I never got to know her children, but I am sure they are beautiful too. I heard from a friend that Aline died of cancer in 2004.

During the time I was in Montreal, Danny kept writing to me, and I got a phone call at least once a week. He also came to visit me two or three times, but for some reason I wasn't that interested. However, since I didn't have many friends in this new city, at least Danny was an enjoyable companion to do things with. At the end of February 1961, I moved back to Rivière-du-Loup, and I was happy to be closer to home.

Things got serious again with Danny. I was working long hours and many nights, so we saw each other in my free time. I was happy. Sometimes he brought some of his friends along and we went to a restaurant together. I had met someone who told me he loved me, and I believed him. However, for some reason, I never met anyone in his family, so I started to have some questions. We never went to the town of Trois Pistoles, where he was living, which was about fifty miles away. That was not too far for a Sunday afternoon drive, but we always went somewhere in the opposite direction.

He was busy a lot of the time; he had bought a garage and told me that he had to work very hard to make sure that the business would be a success. I believed everything he told me. One day I asked to see his place of business. We were on our way, but as we got close, he said that the employees were extremely busy, and if he stopped by, he would have to go to work. I thought that it was a bit peculiar, but like always, I believed him.

Call me stupid ... because I was. I had fallen in love with the man that I thought he was; I was in love with the character of this acting scenario. When I look back at it now, I know that something in the back of my mind was telling me to be more cautious, but my heart took over my common sense. I continued to sense some discomfort with him, but nothing prepared me for the shock I was about to have.

I had been going with him for about two years when I discovered he was married. When I confronted him he denied it. I told the priest of his parish about what I had learned. The priest sent me a letter telling me that there were two men in the parish named Danny, with the same last name, and one was married, the other single. I thought that someone must have made a mistake. I still had some doubt, but thinking that I could trust a priest, I was relieved and resumed the relationship, but I did not have the trust that I usually had.

At the end of September 1962, I started to feel that something wasn't right with me, and in the middle of October, I went to see a doctor and found out that I was pregnant. I was very upset because I had been thinking about terminating the relationship with Danny. It wasn't taking me anywhere, and there wasn't any kind of commitment from him. Especially after those times of incertitude, I had lost interest in him. So I talked to him and told him that I wanted to think about our relationship; he agreed to stay away for a while. About the same time, I got a letter from the same parish priest, telling me that he had made a big mistake. After doing more research, he found out that the Danny I was seeing was married. One Saturday night, his wife and his sister came to visit me at work to confirm what I already knew. I was so confused. I could not believe what was happening to me.

About this time, I was four months pregnant. I called Danny and told him I needed to talk to him. I must have sounded desperate because he came the same day. When I told him about the baby, he was silent for a while and then said it must be someone else's baby because he had an illness that prevented him from reproducing. I was furious because the baby was his and he knew it. After a few more words, I went to my place and decided to plan how to get through this time without letting anyone know what was going on in my life. I kept it a secret from everyone, and this made it a very heavy burden to carry alone.

After I told Danny about the pregnancy, I ran into him three times. The first was in November 1962, when he showed up for lunch at the restaurant where I was working. He and a new girlfriend sat at my table. I had to serve their food. He had played a dirty trick on me, and it was most upsetting to see them together, but I did my work with my head held high. Now I knew him for who he really was—a very nasty man. I saw him again during the Christmas holiday. He came into the same restaurant for a late snack after a party. This time he was with his wife, the real one, and a mutual friend. Again, he sat at my table, and again I served them. The third time would be the last time, at the end of February 1963.

I planned to move to Quebec to wait for the birth of my baby. Danny was the only one who knew about my pregnancy because I wanted to keep it a secret. I didn't want to tell my parents or anyone, for that matter. I needed a place to live while I was waiting for the baby to be born. I read in the newspaper about a few homes there where a woman could live and work during her pregnancy. I made phone calls to Quebec City before I moved and after many tries, I finally found a place where I could work as a housekeeper for a family. I just needed someone to take me there. That is when I called Danny and asked that he take me to my new place of work in Quebec.

In one week, I left Rivière-du-Loup after telling everyone that I had found a job in the city and I would be back in the spring.

Without any more explanation to anyone, I was gone. When we arrived in Quebec City, Danny had a hard time finding the place, so he gave me five dollars to find a taxi to take me to the house of my new employer. That was all the help I was going to get from him. At this point, I did not want to see him anymore; I was done with him. I still loved him, but I could not take the abuse and the shame of having him destroy my life.

I did housekeeping for ten dollars a week plus room and board, and was able to stay there until one week after I delivered the baby. I sent some of my wages to my parents, as I had always done. I worked for this family for three and a half months. When I finished working each day, I would go to my room to read or just be alone. I had no one to talk to, no resources nor advice to find a way to keep my baby. No one knew of my situation except my employer, who was an alcoholic. Every weekend the man, his wife, and the parish priest played cards at the kitchen table. They all drank a lot. Sometimes, early in the evening, the priest would try to talk me into giving up the baby for adoption. That made me feel awful, and I would retreat to my room and cry.

To make matters worse, late one night when everyone seemed to be in bed, I was awakened by a noise in my room. When I looked up, someone was standing by my bed. Looking at me was the priest who had been playing cards and drinking all evening. It was dark in the room, but I could see his silhouette, and I was terrified. I was too scared to scream, and only a loud whisper came out. All my life I had been told to respect and obey members of the clergy. They had all the power. After a few seconds my desperate look must have scared the priest because he turned around and left the room. I never told my boss about what happened that night because for sure I would not be believed. I barricaded my door after that incident.

I began making plans for after the baby's birth. I called government agencies and answered newspaper ads. Some people were not very accommodating, others just rude. I had come to Quebec thinking that in a large city it would be easier to get both help and a better job that would pay more after the birth. That shouldn't take too much time, with the experiences I now had. I would be able to afford the living expenses for my baby and me. I had heard stories about other women doing well in the city, being able to support their children, but after some time, I gave up trying to find a solution around Quebec City. It was no better than the small towns I had left.

It took me a while, but I made a choice. I had decided to keep the child. I didn't want Danny to be involved in my life in any way, at any price. I decided that I would return closer to home after the baby's birth and somehow find a way to make it without help. I knew it would not be easy, but I could do without luxuries; I was used to living that way. I was ready, but it turned out to be impossible to achieve that without some help. It was quite depressing to be in that kind of situation.

Late in the evening on June 10, 1963, I started to have cramps. The lady of the house took me to the Hôpital de l'Enfant Jesus in a suburb of Quebec City. I didn't know anything; I wasn't told what to expect about labor and delivery. I was petrified. Two young male doctors at the hospital were in charge of delivering my baby. After a night of pain, they put me to sleep. I was in a panic, but I didn't have much choice.

Martine was born in the evening, June 11, 1963. I had been sedated for a day. This was my first pregnancy, and my small body made for a hard delivery. When I woke up, I asked the nurse to show me my baby, but as she was bringing her to me, a social worker stopped her and said that I wasn't to see the baby without her permission. She wanted me to sign some papers before I saw my child. I remember that the woman had short black hair, was not very slim, and had freckles all over her face. She was an ugly woman!

I cried and refused to sign them. I could not get up because I was too weak from being cut for the delivery, and I was still sedated.

She wanted me to make a decision about my baby, so she sat in a rocker by my bed for a few days just to intimidate me. It was torture for me at that point because I didn't have any idea how I would be able to take care of an infant, but I didn't want to give her up. I had made a plan to keep my baby no matter what happened. I was stubborn and didn't want to change my mind. I knew I could take care of my baby, just as many other women had done before me. I wanted to get out of that place and start working at being a mother. I knew that it would be the end of my freedom, and that I would dedicate most of my time to my baby, who would be dependent only on me.

After a week, the staff changed its tactics and the social worker gave up. I had been sleeping a lot, so finally they stopped the medication, and I was awake most of the time. I had no one to talk to for advice, but a decision had to be made. The nurse finally told me that if I signed the papers, the hospital would keep the baby for six months in the orphanage to give me a chance to get back on my feet. At any time during that period, they said I could come see my child and make my final decision. I told the hospital that I would get a job and come back. I was in the hospital for seven days altogether.

The hardest time of my life was yet to come: the day I was ready to leave the hospital. My recovery took longer than I expected and after a week of agony, I had to leave my baby there. I wasn't allowed to see her before I left and I never knew why, because I had signed papers they told me were temporary. At that point, I wasn't too secure and was mostly anxious to get to work and get my life together. I was worried about the future. I felt that I had lost my freedom, and now I had to worry about how to take care of my baby when I got her back. I had to find a way to get a roof over our heads. I had survived all these years, and I would make it again.

I returned to the family I worked for, stayed one more week to recuperate, and then packed up my belongings that had been left in storage in the boss's basement. I left Quebec City by bus for Rimouski, a town where nobody knew me and I didn't know anyone. On arrival, I went to eat in a Chinese restaurant. At the end of my meal, I asked to speak to the boss about a job. I started work the next day, just two weeks after I had my baby. The job paid only sixty cents an hour, but the tips were great, and the boss always gave me an extra five dollars every payday because I was such a good worker.

At the boss's recommendation, I rented a room from a woman who had an unmarried sister with two children, so I felt safe that she would understand my situation when it became necessary. When I finally got Martine, perhaps she would babysit for me while I was at work—then I would be able to survive with my baby. Things were going well, but nothing was perfect, and I took a day at a time. I was lonely, but hope kept me going. I had been brought up poor and had survived, so I probably could do it again. And I felt safe out of the reach of Danny; I didn't ever want to see him again.

After working at the Chinese restaurant in Rimouski for about two months, I was ready to go back to the hospital to pick up my baby. During that time I didn't visit her so I could save my money for later when she would be with me. With enough money saved I decided it was time to go arrange to get her back. On my next day off, I left early in the morning by bus to the orphanage in Quebec City. I had made a few preparations for the return trip to Rimouski with my baby, but I had a strange feeling. I didn't like having her moved to the orphanage instead of keeping her in the hospital where I had hoped she would be kept, so I didn't buy too many things. I wanted her back, but I had an instinctive feeling that I might not return with her. I was feeling apprehensive, thrilled, and scared all at the same time.

When I arrived at the orphanage in Quebec, I got off the bus in front of a large gray building that sat at the top of two sets of steep stairs. This large structure had a sad and authoritative feeling surrounding it, which gave me a feeling of loneliness. I climbed the steps, opened the large door, and just felt that I finally had made it this far. I was full of hope.

I went to the desk in front of the entrance, introduced myself to the receptionist, and told her why I had come. She gave me a less-than-warm welcome and told me to take a seat and wait. I waited for a long time before I inquired about the delay. She told me that the staff was very busy. As I sat, some of the people passing by would look at me, but continue on their way without a word. I started to panic. Lunchtime came. Finally, I was told that someone was to talk to me after lunch. I felt relieved. After lunch, I was still waiting and more worried, so I stopped nuns and nurses and asked when someone would talk to me. Where was my baby? No one knew what I was talking about.

After almost a day of begging, finally a nurse took me to a separate room and proceeded to tell me that a good family had adopted my baby and it was too late for me to do anything. She already had a home. I could not believe it. I thought it was my punishment. They told me that the papers I had signed gave them permission to have my child adopted. They said that I could not get any information of any kind because it was the law and it was final. The hospital had lied to me. I had some bad feelings about this situation because it had been so hard to talk to someone at the orphanage whenever I called. I could never get a straight answer all during those two months of waiting as her mother.

Later I found out that my daughter had not been adopted yet, but was in the orphanage in the same building where I was looking for her that day. She stayed there for another two months until she was adopted.

When I left the hospital, I was in a state of shock. I went out of the building through the same door that I had entered that morning. As I walked down the stairs, I had the feeling that everyone was looking at me. When I reached the bottom of those gray stairs, I turned and walked away from their view. I didn't want them to see me crying. I don't remember how I passed those few hours that I had to wait for the bus that would take me home. I sat in the back of the bus and cried all the way to Rimouski. I didn't want anyone to know that I was such a failure. I thought of myself almost as a criminal to have my daughter taken away from me. I should have fought back with more energy, but it was too late. I discovered that my only recourse was to wait until my daughter turned twenty-one, but then I would be too old to be in her life to be a mother to her.

Once again, I had a door slam in my face, and this time the door had dashed all my options. It was final. I had no recourse, and I was too embarrassed to ask anyone for help. I don't know why I didn't try to see a lawyer or seek someone's help. Perhaps I was numb from too many deceptions. I didn't trust anyone. So many people had lied to me.

For a while, I was terribly sad on the inside, but I got used to the situation because this was not the time to be depressed. I tried to keep on going as if everything were normal. I didn't want anyone to feel sorry for me. It took a while, but I was such a good actor that no one ever knew how I felt in my heart. Everything reminded me of my child. On special days like Christmas or my daughter's birthday, I was very sad and just wanted to buy Martine a gift. I prayed that she had good parents.

I returned to work, and although I was sad, I was used to deception and threw myself into my work, trying to forget the past.

I had been working about six months when Danny reappeared in my life. He was waiting outside the door at the end of my shift. He was right there in front of me and wanted to talk to me. After an argument, we agreed to talk the next day.

When we did meet, he just wanted to know if I would be interested in reconciling. I got upset and said, "Go to hell!" He slapped my face. It stung but I ignored it until an hour later when I got home, looked in the mirror, and saw a red spot on my forehead. That was the last time I ever talked to Danny. I knew it would be difficult, but I was determined to make a new life for myself and maybe later find my daughter. If a person hasn't gone through this sort of trauma in her life, it is hard to understand.

I have forgotten many things about those days, perhaps because I wanted to forget that part of my life, but it was always in the back of my mind. Everything reminded me of my daughter, especially any little girl. I was on the lookout for any small child that might look like me.

I finally stopped looking for her and decided to change jobs. I moved back to Quebec City, where I got a job in another restaurant. I'd told everyone that I was going to Toronto in an effort to learn English. I just wanted peace and something of a normal life. Danny had taken all the trust I had in everybody and twisted it in so many ways. I will be forever damaged by what he did to me.

Martine's birth had changed my life forever. It took me a long time to get back on track. I constantly made phone calls to all kinds of agencies for help, and every time I was told the same thing in so many words: It was the law, and I had no recourse. Depression and shame set in for many years. I also experienced a feeling of rejection by the public, but it was probably only in my imagination.

I never told anyone about my despair until I married Henry, my first husband. My marriage to Henry on March 25, 1969, brought some hope to me, and when I got pregnant with Angela, it was a relief and a joy. I do love children, so having Martine with me would have been so special, but since I couldn't have her, I was going to be a good mother to Angela, and I was the best I could be.

Many years later, I told my sister Gisele about Martine. By then, Martine was getting close to her twenty-first birthday, and I still had not found her, despite all my attempts. I even consulted a fortune teller, who was not much help. Gisele helped me find all kinds of agencies through radio programs that tried to reunite families as well as mothers and children. One of the programs featured Jeannette Bertrand who also wrote a column in a popular newspaper in Quebec called *La Patrie*. There were also other agencies doing this kind of research.

After many years of disappointment Henry, Angela, and I decided as a family that one more time I would try to find Martine. It had always been hard on me to get those negative answers, but with help and support, I knew I could and would finally get the answer I wanted.

Chapter 4

Henry

※

Henry Yee emigrated from China to Vancouver, British Columbia, in 1956. He was sponsored by his uncle Lee Moon. He worked as a cook in the restaurant in Rimouski, where I also was working in 1963. We didn't work the same shift, so I didn't know him. One of my coworkers wanted to introduce me to one of her male friends, but I was not interested and told her so. When she told me that her friends had planned an evening at the only nightclub in town, I decided it would be nice to check it out since I had heard that the music was good. The bandleader's last name was Desrosier, and he was from Haiti. He spoke French well and sang and played all our music.

I was able to talk to my friend's friend as the music played. The gentleman was Asian, and he was with his friend Nelson, whom I had been working with for some time in the restaurant. Nelson was a young well-educated Chinese man who had come from China to Vancouver, BC to learn English. For a while, he studied English and bartended at night. He was a smart young man with good manners. Now he was a bit lonely in Ramouski because he was used to big cities like Hong Kong and Vancouver, where the population is largely Chinese.

In 1963 there was a lot of prejudice when it came to relationships, so I decided to let everyone think what they wanted, and I made friends with Nelson's friend Henry. The conversations between us were brief because neither one of us could speak the language of the other. He was Chinese, and I was French.

No one will ever be able to describe completely the feeling and the mystery that occurred when I met Henry. He was a different nationality, and his culture was totally different from mine. I guess that curiosity attracted me to him. I always liked to learn about people and things that were out of my habitual surroundings. It was interesting and somewhat romantic. Now I can sympathize with anyone who has a hard time to be understood for reasons of language and culture.

After a while, our English improved. At first, I had no interest in him, but eventually we became great friends. He always asked me for advice and included me in lots of fun things. We went to movies and dances together. I grew interested in him, but I was so scared and didn't want to get involved with anyone. I was kind to him, but that was all I could do at that point in my life. I think the complete difference in our nationalities attracted us to each other. We eventually fell in love.

Henry was an attractive man, and all the girls liked him. He was such a good character—polite, well mannered, and always laughing. He was also good-looking and well dressed. He had worked in a barbershop for a few years in Hong Kong, and that is where he learned about the latest fashions. He was so different from anyone I had ever known.

Since Henry was Chinese, it was a challenge to learn about his traditions. That was fine with me because I needed someone different, and a challenge it was to know him and respect the

Chinese culture, but I soon learned. Henry and I encountered lots of prejudice. I never knew what the word *prejudice* meant, but I experienced it quickly. Henry and I were rarely seated at the good table in any restaurant; we were whistled at and got mean looks and remarks. We formed our small group of acquaintances, mostly Chinese. They always made me feel welcome. We were in love, and I felt protected and appreciated. I always had Henry's full support for anything I wanted to do. We didn't think twice about all this and kept on going. By that time, we were inseparable, and I knew it was real love.

Henry and I had many good times for three years, until he went back to Vancouver, BC, which was his uncle's city. While on his trip, he wrote to me. I was surprised and happy to hear from him. After a long absence, he came back to Rimouski. I was uncomfortable with him and didn't know why. I felt that he had changed; he was more serious and not the smiling person that he used to be. What had happened to him on his trip?

After a while, he told me that he had been married in Vancouver while on that trip. The wedding had been prearranged in China, the way marriage was done in that country. He did not want to marry that girl, but he felt obligated to his mother and uncle, who had been so good to him. He had gone immediately to a lawyer and sought an annulment of the marriage at any price. It was tough to get a divorce in those days—the only reason was infidelity. It took five years for the divorce to finally go through, and he went through hell, so many difficulties. His wife made him pay for his mistake. But since we were in love, we helped each other through those times.

Henry and I moved to Quebec City from Rimouski early in 1965 and worked at different restaurants, but we spent our days off together. Two years had passed, and his divorce was at a standstill. It was impossible to get things done over the phone. His wife stalled every step of the way. The lawyer told Henry to return to Vancouver if he wanted to get it done. In May, Henry moved back to Vancouver. His friend had two apartments; one became available and was just right for Henry. Before Henry left, we had decided that I would join him later. He wanted to make sure he had a job to help me with living expenses. The opportunity to move to Vancouver came in June 1966.

Henry's friend Nelson was married to my friend Joan, who was French Canadian and a nurse's aide. After being married for two years, they decided to move to Vancouver because of better opportunities there. Joan wanted a female companion with her, so I agreed to take the trip with Nelson and her. We planned the trip for two months. I was technically single at the time, and the idea of a little adventure sounded just perfect for me. Moreover, I was anxious to be with Henry again. The three of us got along well and I decided that I was going to have a good time and enjoy the trip no matter what happened.

At the end of June, we started on our journey to Vancouver with our life savings, which was not much, and all the rest of our belongings in the trunk of Nelson's car. It was an old 1959 Plymouth, plum and beige in color, with no air-conditioning. We left in the afternoon, all excited and maybe a little sad, but we just kept talking about our futures. We planned on finding jobs and made a pact that the first one who found a job would help the other two until all three of us had work.

The first stage of our trip took us to Chicago. Nelson and Joan took turns driving; since I didn't know how to drive, I was at everyone's mercy. We arrived in the Windy City in the early morning. From the bridge, I could see a blanket of fog covering the city's tall buildings. I think it was the smoke coming from all the manufacturing plants. All of a sudden, a feeling of sadness came over me. I felt that I was saying good-bye to a friend. I wanted to cry and turn back, but the excitement of seeing Henry again took over. That feeling of "no return" lingered for the rest of the day. I remember reaching the outskirts of Chicago where we stopped for breakfast at a small café. Most of the patrons eating there were black people, and I realized that it was the first time that I had seen more than two or three black people in the same place. The rest of the day was a bit of a drag because it was raining. We stopped to rest in the early afternoon.

The next morning, Nelson had us on the road before the sun came up. He liked to get an early start, and that was the only part of the trip I didn't like. I never was an early riser, but I got used to his schedule. It was a no-pressure journey. When we saw something of interest, we stopped, sometimes for a day or two. Nelson liked country music and would sing along with the radio or a tape. He sang country songs with a Chinese accent. He had a good voice and had been dancing and acting in show business for some time in Hong Kong. He entertained us as we traveled southwest through Denver, and made our way to Albuquerque, New Mexico, where we stopped at many small shops and purchased souvenirs. The beautiful American Indian salesgirls had long black hair and genuine smiles.

We stopped at a small packed restaurant called Oasis, a good choice for a name because the weather was extremely hot. It was so hot that we had to drive through the desert at night. We got at the end of a caravan of cars that we happened to meet up with. People traveled this way in the desert in case someone had trouble with the heat. We attached a bag of water to the front near the radiator to keep it from overheating during our crossing. Joan was too sleepy and could not stand that kind of heat, so I sat in the front seat of the car to keep Nelson company.

Everyone was buying water or soda to take with them. Joan did not want to wake up. I was a bit worried about her because none of us had ever been in a place that hot before. When you come from Quebec, you can't imagine a place as hot as New Mexico. I had seen cowboy movies with the sand, the scenery, and the cowboys always looking for water holes for the horses, but I didn't know how important it was to pay attention to the water. Now I felt like I was in a real western movie. We had reached the western boundary of the state by early morning when Joan woke up. She had missed all the fun, but I think she was happy about that. As for me, I was wide-awake and amazed at this new adventure of discovery.

By early evening, after traveling west, we were somewhere in Arizona. We decided to stop for something to eat. Nelson began to look in the car for his tiger tails that he had gotten in Canada as a gift from the Shell gas stations when he filled up the tank. Joan and I always watched from far away to detect the Shell sign on this trip. We had bought all the gas so far at Shell stations, and Nelson had gathered quite a few more tails. When he discovered they were missing, he thought maybe we were playing a joke on him. He started to empty the trunk and looked in our luggage to find his tiger tails, but to no avail. He must have dropped them earlier during the trip. I was sitting on the sidewalk laughing so hard. Poor Nelson never found his tiger tails that were souvenirs of Quebec.

Our next stop was Los Angeles. We stayed there for a few days, waiting for some friends who, like us, were traveling across the United States. They were supposed to meet us in LA. They knew the city and planned to show us around. We were a couple of days early so we stayed in a motel at night and visited places during the day. On the third night, someone knocked on the door and said to Nelson, "How much did it cost you for one of the girls?" That motel wasn't for rest only! No need to say that we did not want to stay another moment. We quickly packed our belongings and hit the road. We had heard some bad things about the big city and this must have been one of them.

Early one evening, Nelson decided that we should take a car ride before we went to bed. We had found a new motel and had eaten dinner. Looking at the map, he chose a town that was probably fifty miles from where we were staying! Following the map, he kept on driving until we found ourselves on a two-lane road with not many cars coming or going. It was getting dark, and BEWARE OF BEARS signs were the only ones posted along the road. I didn't know bears roamed in California; I thought their territory was only in the cold places like Quebec, as that is where I had seen them as a child! After some time passed, a long time for me, Nelson wanted to turn around, but a turning place was hard to find on the road because the car was so big. Eventually, we did find a place to turn around and were finally on the way back to Los Angeles. I was never so happy to see city lights again and to be away from signs about bears. Our friends eventually joined us and we shared the "bear stories" with them.

After zigzagging north through California, Oregon, and Washington and stopping to visit friends, we finally arrived in Vancouver, BC one month later, toward the end of July. The city of Vancouver was a large port city, a nice place to live. It was extremely diverse, with a larger cluster of different nationalities, giving it an international feeling. Walking on Robson Street was like being in Germany; Easting Street was like being in a Chinese city. I had only been to Montreal, which had an almost all-white French-speaking population.

We found an old motel on Easting Street, the only place we could afford. We stayed there until we found an apartment. It was the end of July, and we saw FOR RENT signs everywhere, but we had problems finding a place.. Nelson searched throughout the city, but the answer was always the same: "The apartment is already rented." Since Nelson was Chinese, no one wanted to rent to us. This prejudice taught me a good lesson.

Joan and I looked around on our own but had no luck either. We had been in the motel for more than a week, and our money was running low. Nelson had found a job with Henry, but we desperately needed a place to live. Finally, Nelson and Henry learned that one of their friend's parents had two small one-bedroom places that were big enough for two persons in each room. With lots of cleaning, we made the place livable.

Joan decided to go to nursing school. Nelson, Henry, and I found jobs right away in restaurants. I saw a sign in the window of a restaurant: WAITRESS WANTED. I applied for the job and was hired on the spot. The next day I started as a server at Europa Café. It was a good trade to have at that time because there was always a need for employees in that line of work. My boss, Mr. Horstman, and most of the staff were German and spoke that language most of the time, using only a few words of French. I did learn a new language, but it was a mixture of English, French, and German. I became a Yah! Yah! girl, and the accent stayed with me for many years. I was on top of the world. I had a job. *Yeah!*

The move to Vancouver was a big challenge for me. Since I didn't speak English, it was not easy to make myself understood. One day I needed to replenish my nylon stocking supply. (At that time, women wore stockings everywhere.) I tried to buy a pair of stockings at the Bon Marché, a large chain store in Canada, but no one could understand me. I had to go behind the counter and show the clerk what I wanted. Believe me, I was embarrassed! The next week, I was in school learning English for two hours a day. It was a slow and difficult process. I was learning English faster at my job talking with the customers than I was learning at the school. When I finished work about 10 p.m., I would go home and watch Johnny Carson on *The Tonight Show*, which aired on TV at 11:00 p.m. From watching Johnny, I learned English. Thank you, Johnny. It was fun learning from you.

I worked at Europa Cafe for three years and made some friends. The owners loved me because I was always on time, and many of the customers were from Europe and spoke French. I could communicate easily with them. After I had worked at the restaurant for a while, the owner would often leave me in charge if he had had too much to drink and wanted to rest. He had a small trailer behind the restaurant, and during slow times, he would go there to take a nap. Mr. Horstman liked liquor, and he frequently overdid the drinking. He would become very friendly with female customers. I talked to him about it, and he told me to please not let him lose control.

Early one evening he was already getting friendly, and I tried to talk to him, but to no avail. All the staff was walking on eggshells, and I was getting worried that he would do something to get himself in trouble. All the servers kept looking at me to do something, but I was helpless. He was my boss. I got the idea to send him to the trailer to get something we needed. While he was inside, I locked the door from the outside with a large plank. He kicked and yelled when he realized what I had done. Finally, he stopped making a racket. When the restaurant closed for the night, I went back to the trailer, unlocked the door, and ran away as fast as I could.

The next day when I arrived at work, I was a bit apprehensive, but I knew my boss did not want this story to get around. He knew that I would not talk about it, for I was not the type to spread news. I liked to keep those kinds of stories to myself. To my surprise, he was already at work. He didn't say much except, "Rose, thank you for what you did last night." He presented me with a bottle of Blue Nun wine. Not one word was ever said about the incident. When I went back to Vancouver in 1996, I passed by the restaurant and remembered some of those good times. The street had changed a lot, mostly new buildings, but the Europa Café still stood in the same place; the only change was a new facade and, I am sure, many more stories.

In August 1966, when we were settled, the weather was in the nineties, very hot. The city was clean and surrounded by water with beautiful beaches. We lived close to English Bay, a beautiful beach that was always full of people. Almost every afternoon, I would walk to that beach. I had never had a tan in my life, but that year I was the darkest white girl in Vancouver. In the evening, we used to take a ride to Stanley Park, one of the most beautiful parks in the world. The air was so fresh that it gave us a sense of freedom and good health. About halfway into the park, there was a curb service restaurant, a popular hamburger place called *The White Spot*. Many nights we would stop there to get a burger and a milkshake at 11:00 p.m., just before going to bed. Times have changed since then, as has my waistline!

At the time we were living in Vancouver, the west side was the best part of the city, with a choice of the best restaurants and clubs. The nightlife provided a large variety of entertainment, with the best performers in the business. The downtown streets were large, and there was no jaywalking because the fine was heavy. The crime rate was also very low. Vancouver was a fashion-oriented city. Men and women wore suits to work and could be distinguished from ordinary people on the streets who wore more casual attire. The weather was refreshingly mild in the spring. In the summer, the temperature was in the eighties, and there was very little snow in the winter. However, there was lots of rain and fog, especially in the fall. The rest of the summer of 1966 was more like a long vacation. I enjoyed every minute of it.

I made many great friends because of the trip that Nelson, Joan, and I took in the summer of 1966. We still have friends who live in Vancouver, and I visit them from time to time. Because of that trip, my life took a whole new turn and became a real adventure for me. I learned a lot from being away from my old life, and I had reunited with Henry, who was always ready for something new and different.

Nelson, Henry, Joan, and I didn't need many things, because we were working or studying most of the time. But in the end, we had a good time being together.

We had been using Henry's company car from the restaurant where he worked for our travel to and from work for almost a year. One day Henry said to me, "If you get your driver's license, I'll buy you a car." I'm sure you can guess my answer to that! It took me over three months to get my license. I was good at driving, but the written test was a bit of a challenge. Henry kept his promise and bought me my first car, a brand new 1966 Cougar, for three thousand dollars. It was beige with a brown top and a white leather interior. We were proud and liked to show it off. I got to drive it most of the time. Henry drove his company car. Those were the days, my friend!

I was so busy with my life that I didn't miss my family too much, but the holidays were hard for me. I felt lonely away from my family. I had many friends from other countries who felt the same way, so we usually tried to get together and have dinner at each other's homes during the holidays. Because everyone was a bit lonely, we formed a kind of special friendship. That bond of friendship was dear to me. I always loved the closeness of family, and even though my family was poor, I loved my siblings very much. I still do to this day. I am lucky to have a close family even though we live far apart.

After two years in Vancouver, Henry was offered a job in Nanaimo, B.C., across the bay. It wasn't far but it was a remote area on an island, and all transportation was done by boats or planes. Twice a day, a seaplane landed across the street from where we had an apartment. It was beautiful to have that view of the water. It was also noisy.

I took a job at a restaurant in Nanaimo. The owner was Spanish. At that time, I really needed a job, but he was the worst boss I ever had, and I already had some bad ones. He was rude to the employees and so distrusting that everyone was treated like a thief. It was the worst working atmosphere I ever experienced. I had always been honest, and having someone checking my every move made me so nervous that by the time I went home, I was so exhausted I could barely take a bath and go to bed. I swore that if I ever got to be a boss one day, I would never be like him. Later on, I did become the boss of my own business, and I always treated my employees with respect and did the best I could for them. I never felt the guilt or shame from mistreating any other person.

Henry had contacted TB as a young boy in China. He had recovered, but was always bothered by asthma. In Nanaimo, he became very sick once again from asthma. I took him to the hospital. He stayed there for over two weeks and most of the time used a respirator to help him breathe. I was so worried and lost without him. When he got out of the hospital, we decided to move to a cheaper place outside of the town. It was a dump, but it fit our budget. Since I was the only one working for two months, as a waitress, my budget was limited. I was barely making enough to pay for food and rent.

When the holidays came in 1968, Henry and I were alone, and one more time my financial situation was not looking good. If I was fired from my job, I didn't know what we would have done. My boss knew of my situation, and he was exploiting it to the maximum. He made me feel that I was at his mercy as often as possible, but I am not an easy person to discourage. It was a sad Christmas that year.

After the holiday, Henry got much better and returned to work part time. It was a big relief for me. I had applied for another job in the same town. A few weeks later, the owner called and asked if I was still interested in the job. "Oh, yes," I said, and the next day I was at work with a smile on my face. I never gave a notice to my old boss, something I had never done before. It was the only time in my entire life that I was so happy to get a new job. The new job had a fair boss and a happy atmosphere, which made the work enjoyable.

I worked in that restaurant for a few months, and when we had enough money, we moved back to Vancouver and lived in Richard Wong's apartment. He had been a friend whom we met when we first arrived in Vancouver. Richard had been sick and could not go to work. Leanne, his wife, was working at an accounting office, and things were lean. Richard was studying for his license in real estate. Occasionally, I tried to help him, giving him quizzes. He got his license but still wasn't satisfied. Then Henry and Richard decided to start a panel business. They would make panels that you see very often in Asian houses to separate rooms, or to hide a part of the room. Since they both had asthma, their allergies were too powerful for them to continue the fabrication, so they went on to other projects.

I had a job in downtown Vancouver during the time of the hippies. I was working in a hotel across from the city hall and Radio Canada. There was a big fountain in front of the building where the hippies gathered to smoke their pot and bathe in the fountain. We never knew what they were going to do next for attention. From across the street, it was more like an attraction, and no one was too fond of them. The police were busy. As for me, I enjoyed watching all the action!

Henry received a job offer from the United States in 1968, from Benny Kwong. It was an opportunity that he had been talking about for a while. He decided to go for a month to try it. He came back to Vancouver and applied for his green card. At the time, we were more or less engaged, so he wanted me to apply for my green card too. I remember how difficult it was to go through all the tests and the papers. We had to be fingerprinted, and there was no end to the demands. Finally, Henry got his card in March 1969, and I got mine in April of the same year.

We decided to get married before Henry went back to the United States. There was a lot of controversy over our getting married. Some said, "The marriage won't last. Your children will be different." (Yes, they are different. They are educated, intelligent, and drug-free.) My mother even called Henry my "Chinese friend" for over five years and always said, "He will leave you and go back to Hong Kong, and you will never see him again."

We proved everyone wrong. Our relationship was not an overnight affair. We had come to know each other, and trust was one of the main attributes that had kept us together the last few years. We had gone through many difficulties and felt very close to each other. We talked a lot, but we didn't need a long conversation to understand each other. We were so much alike in many ways.

On March 25, 1969, we tied the knot. It was a nice day, but the wedding almost didn't happen. The civil ceremony at the city hall was supposed to start at 9:30 a.m. I was there with two friends, Joan and Rejane, but the groom did not arrive on time. We waited for thirty minutes, and finally he showed up with his witness Chuck. I was almost in tears by that time. Henry and Chuck had decided to go to breakfast on their way to the wedding and didn't think it was so important to be on time. It was humiliating for me, but as always, I kept it to myself and never talked about it again. A few days later, I found out that Henry got cold feet at the last minute; his friend Chuck had to convince him to go ahead with the marriage. It gave me a shock at a time when I was supposed to be happy. I felt that every time I had some joy in my life, it turned out to be pain. I never told anyone about this, but it stayed in my heart all of my life. I never told Henry that I knew about that incident. I tried to forgive and forget.

A few days after we were married, Henry moved to Yakima in

Washington State to work for Benny Kwong, who owned a large restaurant in a large hotel. It featured a floor show and popular music. I joined Henry six weeks later. I had to stay behind because my immigration papers took longer to prepare. Once again, I had to leave my friends and the small amount of familiarity that I had acquired in Vancouver. The only things I took with me were my clothes and a small radio. All my other possessions were left behind.

The restaurant was a busy place. Henry worked in the kitchen, and I was a waitress. I made sixty cents an hour plus tips. Henry was paid six hundred dollars a month plus room and board for both of us. There was no air-conditioning in our room. Coming from the lower temperatures of Quebec, I had no tolerance for heat, and that first summer was hell; the temperature reached 120 degrees inside as well as outside during the day. I tried to work long hours, and during my time off, I would go to the library because it was air-conditioned. We worked long hours but didn't care; we were trying to save some money.

The second summer was even worse. I was skinny and used to go the pharmacist across the street to get a food supplement to gain weight. Starting in July, almost every morning I was getting sick, so I decided to see a doctor; maybe the heat was too much for me. To my surprise, I was pregnant. The doctor gave me a prescription for my morning sickness. When I took it to the pharmacist, he told me with a smile that I no longer needed the food supplement to gain weight.

Henry was happy with the news, and we talked about the future and the plan for a family. I was on cloud nine, but I was also sick the entire nine months. A few weeks before the birth, a woman who had befriended me had a baby shower for me. Her name was Yvonne; she was a delightful person. I was surprised and happy. It was the first time in my life that someone had done something so special for me. I had so many gifts; I took the boxes home in disbelief.

On February 25, 1971, our daughter was born. I had been a little worried during my pregnancy because I knew of a Chinese custom of having a boy for the first child. I'd wondered how Henry would react if we had a daughter, but he loved our baby girl.

I remember that when I told Henry we had a little girl, he said, "Now we have a little queen with us." We named her Angela Linda Yee. We both loved that name, and for a long time we called her Angel. Henry adored her and came home every night during his break to check on her. It was the best time of my life. We took her everywhere we went; she was such a good baby. She had her father's Asian looks and dark hair—and my big brown eyes. I kept her well dressed in the clothes I sewed. I was good with my sewing machine and could make just about anything. I made most of my clothes, and it was even more fun to make things for a baby.

We had moved to a new apartment in the same hotel. It had two rooms; one served as a kitchen and the other was a bedroom with a bathroom. The kitchen had a small table and two chairs. It also had a shelf that I used for my electric hot plate. Henry decided to buy a TV because no one would babysit for us without something to pass the time. Angela liked to watch it too.

I had to go back to work when Angela was three months old. I worked all night downstairs in the restaurant so I could be with her during the day. A teenage girl babysat for us, but I would check on Angela during the evening. Sometimes it was hard to manage sleep, but I didn't care. I had my little girl with me; I wasn't alone anymore.

I had been so alone for those last two years, living in one bedroom and out of boxes, with no one to talk to. Henry was working long hours, so most of my time was spent alone, at work, or at the library. I had a small radio that only played a few stations, not much for entertainment. I could have used a TV during those long days and nights.

When Angela was one and a half years old, we left Benny Kwong and Yakima and moved back to Vancouver for eleven months. Henry worked for a friend, and I worked in a restaurant until we moved to Portland, Oregon, in 1973, where we leased the Barbur Tower restaurant. This business was good but required long hours from both of us. We had to take Angela to a babysitter every day. After a few months, Angela complained about being left alone in the dark at the babysitter's. I thought I had found a woman with a good reputation. She was the wife of the school principal and had three boys and a girl. The girl was the youngest of the children, about the same age as Angela. She said that she wanted a companion for her little girl to play with.

After a while, I decided to check out Angela's story by making an unannounced visit one evening. I had a key to get in the babysitter's house because I worked late hours. I found Angela alone in the family room in the basement. I picked her up, took her home, and never had contact with the sitter again. She never contacted me either to find out why I had removed Angela from her home. After that, we kept Angela with us in the restaurant while we worked. This way we knew she was safe.

Our assistant chef had expressed his desire to buy the restaurant, so we decided to sell the business to him. After the deal was settled, the three of us got in the car for a long ride, and it felt so good to be free and be a family again.

We moved back to Yakima, and Henry worked at Kioke, a Chinese restaurant there. I worked part time at another restaurant, organizing banquets as well as waiting tables. I also had to work late sometimes. By then, Angela was four years old, and a coworker's daughter babysat for us. I felt secure having her with Angela, and Angela loved her.

Angela started school in Yakima and did well. I never had to push her. At five, she took gymnastics and did some modeling for a while. She was at ease at big modeling shows, doing exactly what she was told to do. I was so proud of her. She also took piano lessons for four years. As always, she did well. She enjoyed roller-skating and was involved in many activities. It wasn't always easy for me because of my work schedule.

When Angela was six years old, we sold our duplex in Yakima for sixty-four thousand dollars, and with a profit of twenty-one thousand dollars, we moved to Port Angeles in the fall of 1977, where we opened a restaurant in February 1978.

Owning a restaurant had been our longtime dream, but it didn't happen overnight. We worked every day for three months, from the end of October to the beginning of February. The place was filthy; it had been used as a pool hall and only served beer. Henry and I scrubbed every corner of the place. The bar was all black, but when I started to clean it, I discovered that there was mahogany under all that gummy dirt. It took me almost a week to clean the wood. When we finally finished cleaning everything, it didn't look like the same place. We had to wait for the liquor license and some money from a bank loan, which took forever to arrive. We were scared that we would run out of money for everyday living.

Angela didn't have much that Christmas. I sewed a few clothes for her and made her a stuffed cat. She kept the cat for a long time. We had Christmas dinner at Linda and Vaughn's house; they were friends and they too were far from their families. We were happy to be with each other for this holiday.

Henry always found time to do things with Angela. One day I went shopping, and while I was out, as usual, they liked to play like two boys. He taught her some karate kicks, and they used to move the furniture and have a round of karate. That day when I got home, they both had guilty looks, but they were watching TV, so I didn't pay much attention. A few days later, I noticed that my small antique table was missing so I asked them where it was. They exchanged guilty looks and confessed that they'd hit the table with one of their kicks. For a few minutes, I was annoyed, but I decided that their time together was more important than a small table. We had good laughs about it over the years.

Finally, on Friday, February 8, 1978, at four o'clock in the afternoon, we opened the doors to our restaurant, Henri Yee's Orientale, hoping that we would have customers. By six o'clock, we had a full house, and people waited in line for at least an hour. We were ecstatic that all our hard work had paid off. That weekend, Henry and I worked three days without much sleep. By then, we were running on only our nerves. We planned to close on Mondays. The opening had taken us by surprise. We had a few friends who volunteered to help us for a few days. Thanks to them, we were able to survive.

Henry and I were good partners. He ran the kitchen, and I ran the front. In no time, we were on our feet, and what had started as a small restaurant for about one hundred people grew so fast that we added a piano bar in another part of the building after about six months.

After three years of owning the restaurant, Henry gave me a Cadillac for Christmas. I, once a little girl who was always angry, now had a thriving business and a Cadillac. What more did I need! I hired a few of the best people I could find, thanks to the experiences I had from working for others and learning from the mistakes they had made. After a year, we were the talk of the town. The ever-growing business needed more room to accommodate our ever-growing clientele. In the larger bar that we added, we hired a good band to play.

A few famous TV actors came in to enjoy a good meal; Daddy Warbucks from the cast of *Little Orphan Annie* came in many times.

The crew of the movie *An Officer and a Gentleman* came for dinner when they were filming about thirty miles from the restaurant.

I was going all day and all night, until two or three in the morning. I was always exhausted, but we were happy; our dream was coming true. We had a nice house, and I even had a housekeeper, which I never dreamed would be possible. Angela was growing up, and we had well-trained employees. I was so proud of myself. Finally, we had accomplished something worthwhile.

Every year, we closed the restaurant for the month of January. The small town had two main industries, a sawmill and a port. It was a tradition to close the sawmill during the month of January. In one way or another, everyone had a job that had something to do with those two industries. This made January a slow month, so we used that time for vacation.

Chapter 5

My Trip to China

❧❦

As a young child, I was fascinated with Chinese culture, the language, and the traditional costumes. Perhaps this interest began because of all the picture books I was exposed to in school. However, I only recognized the French language. If someone spoke to me in another language, it was usually English, because I lived close to the border of Edmunston, a partly English-speaking city. But I never had to learn English because Edmunston was a dual language (French and English) city. During World War II, two English-speaking soldiers stopped and asked me for directions, but I could not understand them. I told my parents that the soldiers spoke to me in Chinese! At that time, I could not imagine that many years later I would be married to a Chinese man, Henry Yee. The Chinese language and traditions intrigued me. Henry told me many stories about growing up in China.

In 1952, when Henry was fifteen years old, he left the village of Toysan just before the Mao Tse Tung regime took over in China. Leaving China at that time was considered treason. Soon the borders were closed to incoming and outgoing traffic. A few days before the final closing, Henry took a chance and left his country.

He left just in time because after the closings, anyone and everyone who tried to leave or enter China was captured, and some were put in prison. Henry went to Hong Kong, to an uncle who had a barbershop in the city. He took Henry in as an apprentice and trained him as a barber, cutting and styling hair for men. Henry also learned about a better way of life while living in Hong Kong because it was a modern city even at that time. Only a few miles away, life was very different.

In those days of the Cultural Revolution, China was a cruel place to live. The days of freedom, when the children were playing outside, singing, and laughing, were gone. Women, children, and a few old men attended the rice fields. Everyone was insecure, no one trusted anyone, voices were kept low, and a look of desperation was on the face of every person. There were no more happy noises from the children, just whispers coming from those little bodies, a look of sadness on all those small faces. The grandparents, too old for the hard work that the fields required, were left at the family home to care for the small children. The living conditions were primitive. Most of the homes had hearth floors made of a mixture of stone and cement. The cooking was done on a large fire pit inside the house, and smoke rose through a special chimney, leaving the inside of the house free of smoke. The people slept on braided straw mattresses that were not very comfortable.

China was a man's world; women did not have many choices. It was more of a tradition then a rule. Women did not ask for control; they did not expect much because of the old Chinese tradition. Expectations were not high, making everyday life more acceptable. The young men and the fathers had gone to fight a war that was imposed on them; the females had to survive alone with the children.

One story in particular was troubling to me. From Henry's parent's house in the valley, they could see groups of Japanese soldiers on the mountaintop, keeping watch on the small farms below. One day his mother had to go on foot to the village for some medicine, and it took her three days to come back because the Japanese soldiers were everywhere. On the way home, she had to make many detours to avoid being captured. People were kept hostage on their own land. There were stories of rape, murder, imprisonment, and torture of those who ventured outside of the guarded area. This environment was war in a very brutal way.

Money was nonexistent; it was a time of bartering. A few people had some pieces of gold that were hidden for a time of extreme situations. Sometimes a family was lucky and the man of the house went to Canada or the United States to work in a restaurant or on the railroad, making a little money for his family in China. It was such a privilege to have someone who cared enough to send money home. Maybe someday he would be able to send for his family and give them a life they always had hoped for, in a land of freedom and abundance that everyone talked about.

Henry was the youngest one in his family. He, his two sisters, and a brother grew up during this dark period of war. His brother later died of tuberculosis at the age of forty-three. His mother was a tiny woman and the matriarch of the family. After the death of her husband, she took on his role in the family, the ruler. Any important decision had to meet with her approval. This meant that no decision was made without her approval, and she didn't hesitate to say no, but when she said yes, her orders were executed without hesitation.

My husband had barely known his father, as he was five years old when his father left for San Francisco, California, to work on the railroad tracks. The family home was larger than most in the village because his father had provided for his family with the money he made in the United States.

Henry often spoke about the respect and support among

members of a Chinese family. Most everything was done as a family project. No one was alone; work, money, and glory were shared.

By 1979, Henry had not seen his mother or family since he'd left China twenty-seven years earlier. His mother was aging, and the time to visit was growing short. He wanted to see her at least one more time and show her his family. On January 2, 1979, Henry, Angela, and I flew from Seattle, Washington, to Hong Kong.

My husband had been brought up in Toysan, a remote village deep in China, from which he had fled as a teenager. Before this visit, he had not been able to return to China because those who returned might be accused of treason, and it was too dangerous to take a chance. Now we could go inside the country without the fear of not coming out, because there was a new regime. This government had changed some of the laws after many years of protest by the Chinese people as well as countries around the world.

It was a long trip. The roaring sound of the plane's engines made everyone sleepy. After a few movies, the ride became more and more tiring. We finally arrived in Hong Kong in the early afternoon of January 3. I wasn't prepared for such a cold, businesslike atmosphere. It was definitely the most controversial place I had ever visited in my life. Today it has changed and become a bit more sociable.

When we arrived at the airport, we had to go through customs. In 1979, the security was still very tight. Henry thought he could be our interpreter, as he knew a few Chinese dialects. However, they chose to use Mandarin dialect, the one my husband was the least familiar with. After getting through the interrogation, we still had to wait while they checked for any false declarations or documents.

I have to say that the Chinese government workers' way of doing business was much different from what I was accustomed to. They worked in a quiet way, and there were few distractions. The blank looks on their faces seemed to imply that they only desired to accomplish their commanders' orders. Every move was calculated. Nothing was done spontaneously.

A government worker had taken our passports and other papers into another room. I was extremely nervous as we waited. There was no comfort in the business office, just a few straight-backed chairs along the walls. Guards everywhere looked at us with their straight faces; if we were to wait for a smile from them, we would have to wait a long time. Not one of them smiled the entire time we were waiting to be processed. Our daughter, Angela, was eight years old at the time. She was a friendly child and was smiling at the guards, but no one was smiling back at her. I sensed that she was getting uncomfortable and a bit scared; she had moved closer to her father.

Finally, to our relief, all our papers were deemed to be in order and were returned to us. They told us that we were free to leave; they had certainly made the process difficult. It had been a long two hours. As soon as we had our papers and our passports in our hands, we grabbed our luggage, got a taxi, and started on our way to the hotel. The ride was not very long, but it was an intense drive, zigzagging around other cars and pedestrians alike. I was amazed that we made it alive to the Hotel Sheraton; our first few hours in Hong Kong was an experience I will not soon forget.

By the time we got to our hotel room, it was getting dark. A servant accompanied us on the elevator to the tenth floor. The room was beautiful, much like the hotels we find here in the States. We had a beautiful view of Hong Kong late at night. Tired and hungry, we needed room service. A waiter was assigned to our room, a young man who was dressed in white from head to toe. This waiter made it clear that he would be at our service all night, and his words proved to be true. He knocked at our door every five minutes, asking if he could bring us something else. With every knock, he had something for us, including fruit, tea, dinner, and drinks. I was getting annoyed; we needed some privacy. At one point in the evening, he came with towels and a choice of oil and soap on a large tray. Later he returned and drew a bath for us. I told my husband to get him out of the room. I needed sleep, not attention. Finally, we got some peace and quiet.

Early the next morning, we went down to the large hotel dining room. It was a busy place, and the waiters had looks of confusion on their faces. The breakfast was mainly Chinese pastry and lychee nuts. There was a choice of coffee or the traditional tea. Henry, Angela, and I were accustomed to this kind of food, so we enjoyed every bite.

Around noon, we planned to meet Henry's younger sister, her husband, her daughter, and an aunt at a popular restaurant. I could not remember any of their Chinese names, even though Henry had told them to me many times. At the restaurant, we were finally seated at a table close to the sidewalk. It was noisy, but we all enjoyed the brouhaha. I could tell that the relatives remarked and snickered about the passersby. My sister-in-law's husband did not participate in the loud conversation, but he did look at every gesture we made. My daughter and I tried new food but only with the approval of my husband. He made sure that what we ate was palatable. I had heard stories about strange food and didn't want to eat anything exotic.

After our long meal, we went by bus with Henry's aunt to her home. We arrived at the front of a five-story apartment building in the middle of the city. The lobby was rather dark and small. The aunt rang for the elevator. All the passengers got off when the door opened. Those waiting to get on made room for her and us too, but not one of them stepped into the elevator. I asked my husband why this was happening, and he said that all those people were tenants, and it would have been a lack of respect to travel in the same elevator with our aunt, who was the owner of the building. She was considered to have status because she was the owner, "a person of affluence". In China, money is power.

When we got to Henry's aunt's apartment on the top floor, I was surprised by the modest appearance of the first room that I saw, a combination living and dining room. There were some nice pieces of furniture, a sofa, some high-back chairs, and a table, all with a black lacquer finish. Some may call the furniture antique, but I called it old. The aunt served us traditional tea and small egg pies. Since I didn't understand much of the Chinese language, I had many surprises ahead of me.

In the elevator, the aunt had told us that she had a balcony, a luxury in the city. I could not believe my eyes when she motioned my daughter and me to follow her to that balcony. She had a big smile on her face as she told my husband that she had a pet. Angela and I followed her out the glass door to the balcony and onto a concrete floor. There was a roof above and screens on all sides, providing a comfortable four-by-four outdoor room. A small straw cage sat in one corner, and there we saw it: a large orange rooster that flapped its wings when we approached. It was the size of a turkey. My daughter thought it was the funniest thing ... but not her mother! Believe me, I was raised on a farm and saw many roosters, but this one made a huge impression on me. It was the largest rooster I had ever seen! My husband had a good time with this surprise, but at times during the visit, Henry had his limits too. He now was Americanized, and he liked his style of living.

The next day, we went by taxi to meet Henry's other sister; she lived in another part of Hong Kong in an apartment with her husband. When his sister opened the door, they grinned at each other. Her two grown children were also there to meet us. There was no kissing or hugging, just a few tears and loud, excited voices full of joy. After meeting everyone, we all went to visit some places of interest in the city. We had lunch at an outside café, and the rest of the afternoon was spent visiting places in my husband's old Hong Kong neighborhood, where he had worked for three years in his uncle's barbershop. It was no longer there, replaced by another business. Hong Kong was an interesting city to visit. It did look busy—everywhere we went, there was a business atmosphere—but we did spend a pleasant few days there.

Early the next day, we departed for Toysan with Henry's sister, her husband, and her daughter. We rented a small van that was driven by a Chinese man. The road to Toysan was bad; in China, when they say country road, they mean it. It would be a long ride. We reached the city of Canton at about lunchtime, and the traffic there was unbelievable. I had never seen anything like it before. We waited for the signal so we could move on the street. I watched cars zigzag through a crowd of bicycles, hundreds of them going in all directions. Most of the riders were wearing white shirts that I assumed were some kind of uniform provided by the government at the time. I watched the scene in amazement; it is almost impossible to describe. There was so much confusion that I could not tell if the vehicles were going backward, forward, or sideways. While all this was happening, a police officer in an all-white uniform, except for black boots, stood on a large cement block in the middle of the intersection, directing the traffic, whistling and screaming. Finally, we had the right of way. I'd thought that we would never get out of that intersection. After a few minutes of driving away from the madness, I was delighted to see our driver park the van in front of a restaurant.

We ate lunch in an overcrowded café. Then we quickly got out of Canton and continued our trip on rural dirt roads up mountains and through ravines. In the early afternoon, we stopped at a village to rest for a few minutes. A shoe shiner had set his stand there, and since I was wearing high red boots, Henry suggested that I give him some business. I sat on a small bench and he proceeded to clean my boots. In an instant, I was surrounded by about fifteen people, mostly children, with their faces very close to mine. It must have been the first time that they saw a woman with blonde hair. I felt a bit uncomfortable. I was happy to get back in the van.

We continued our journey and finally arrived at our destination, the village of Toysan, late in the afternoon. On the road to the village, I was apprehensive. Toysan sits near the bottom of a hill. Looking around, I sensed sadness coming from all directions. There were no flowers and not many trees close to the road. A few trees mostly surrounded large plots of farming land rising on the hill behind the houses. They seemed to be used as a line to separate each landowner's property. The streets of Toysan itself were lined with small houses and larger buildings with apartments where families lived. Those larger buildings were made mostly of dark gray cement, inside and out, and they served as housing for regular government employees.

We drove up to the house where my husband was raised. The house was square with a few small windows. It was somewhat larger than the other houses in the area, but that was the only difference. The door was smaller than what I was used to seeing at home. It was made of a heavy material and painted red like all the neighboring doors and window frames.

Henry's nieces and nephews were waiting outside for us. They took us into the house, where his mother was waiting just inside the door. She took Henry by the hand, led him to a chair, and sat beside him. Again there was loud talk and tears in everyone's eyes, including mine. The talking was continuous. It reminded me of home, when families get together for a special occasion. I restrained myself from asking Henry for a translation, as he could barely keep up with the Chinese conversations. We were invited to sit at a large table and were served tea and individual Chinese egg pies, which

Henry, Angela, and I enjoyed. The nephews drank whiskey but didn't offer me any. Let me tell you, I could have used one of those drinks after such a long drive.

After some time spent talking, dinner was served. Henry's mother commanded the serving of the meal. The men sat first, and the nieces served the men when they gestured for anything. Since visitors were special, we were served first at the table. While Henry's mother was waiting on the side, I asked my husband if I could invite his mother and sister to sit with us at the table. He told me to go ahead and do what I thought seemed right to me, and to forget about the traditions. The few words of Chinese that I knew came in handy when I asked them to sit with us. They all had big smiles on their faces. From that moment on, I acted like an American woman, and I could tell that they appreciated our way of doing things. I listened to them and tried to understand what they were saying; they knew some English words, so we somewhat understood each other.

As the evening turned dark, a light was turned on, a single bulb hanging from the ceiling in the middle of the main room. There was another light in the bedroom, and when it was time for bed, we were assigned one bed for the three of us, with no question about it. Since we were five hours from the nearest hotel, the choice was easy. We would make the best of it. The mattress was made of braided straw and was about half an inch thick, placed on a wooden board. Thanks to my husband, we had brought with us a thick comforter, so we placed it on the top of the mattress. In my childhood, I didn't have a very good bed, but I never slept on that kind of bed before. Maybe that's why the Chinese are up so early in the morning! Sleeping at my mother-in-law's home in Toysan was the only time that I truly remembered looking forward to getting up in the morning. In fact, I was never the last one up for that entire week!

The next morning when we awoke, a niece was already cooking breakfast. The markets opened at the first light of day, and she had already gone there to get what was needed to make breakfast. The cooking area was a four-foot brick square built on large flat rocks at the edge of the kitchen. She cooked *hombow*, a Chinese pastry, on an open fire similar to the BBQ pits that we have in parks. At the bottom, cinder covered the rocks. Over the pit was a bar that reached from one side to the other, with hooks to hold the pots. Even in those primitive conditions, I have to say that she managed to make an excellent meal. During the second day of our visit in Toysan, we spent the time talking and visiting with friends and family. The families were large, and friends came from everywhere.

On the third day, Henry visited his other sister, who lived about four miles from his mother's house. All the family went except for Henry's mother, who was eighty-three years old and wanted to stay at home. Everyone got on bicycles for the ride, except me. One of the nephews had a moped and offered to let me ride with him. I accepted with pleasure, since I did not know how to ride a bike. I sat on the back of the moped, and we were on our way, driving along a busy road filled with other bicycles. I noticed that everyone was staring at me. Suddenly, I realized that I probably was the only blonde-haired person in that area. When one guy turned his head to take a second look at me, he lost his balance, hit the side of the road, and ended up in a ravine with his bicycle. Thank God the ravine wasn't too deep. It gave me the giggles, and I couldn't stop laughing. I had to wait until we got to our destination to explain the crazy laugh I had for half of our ride.

At this sister's apartment house, there was another invitation for dinner waiting for us. Henry's sister, her husband, and their five sons lived in an apartment on the second floor; two steep flights of stairs took us there. The living room was a bit bigger than the usual size. There was a brown couch at each end of the room, a few straight-backed chairs, and a table against the wall, seating six. A shelf where dishes were stored was attached to the wall and extended partway over the table. My brother-in-law and his wife were each wearing a gray cotton suit that looked like a doctor's scrubs. It must have been some kind of uniform since they worked for the government as schoolteachers. I could not understand the language, but I knew they were talking about work, Mao Tse Tung, and the USA. I could tell that they wanted to know more about us, but whatever Henry was telling them, they didn't say much. His sister did some of the talking, but her husband's hums and nods were the only acknowledgement given to Henry.

Henry's sister also had a daughter who was married and had a young son. She came to visit before dinner, later taking me to her apartment for few minutes. It was next door to her parents and was also small and gray. She spoke better English and was understandable. She wore the Red Guard uniform, a navy two-piece suit; her husband and her small son had the same attire. She told me that she was in the Red Army Guard for a while, but now that she had a child, she wasn't involved as much. She also told me that she couldn't have any more children, because of the "one-child" law in China. She gave me a sad look and turned away as if she wanted to change the subject. Most of the visit she had a beautiful smile; her small-framed body was full of life. Her personality reminded me of Henry's, and it made me smile as I thought that they all shared this family trait.

The fourth day, we visited Henry's father's grave. The family plots were on the hill behind the family home, about half a mile from the house. His father was buried there. That spot had the best view of the surrounding area, and everyone from this family would be buried there. It is the custom to bring food instead of flowers to the grave; my daughter was assigned the honor. I watched her climbing the small hill and thought about how she would never get to know this man that everyone called "gung gung", which means grandfather in Chinese. I didn't have much time with my grandfather, but I had a few good memories of him. My daughter would never get those sweet memories of her "gung gung".

Henry's father had always wanted to take his family to California with him one day, but when he came back to get the family eight years later, he contracted tuberculosis. This was a common illness at the time, and since the medicine wasn't very good then, it usually meant death for anyone who contracted the illness. So this poor man who had worked so hard for his dream was never able to see it fulfilled. He died shortly after he returned home. However, Henry made the decision that he would try to carry out his father's dream. I am glad that he did!

The last evening before our departure, the family was quiet. Henry sat in a chair beside his mother; he was her baby. She looked at him with the eyes of a proud mother. She was the strong one, shedding only a few tears during that long night. The others sat around us with anxious looks on their faces, not smiling much, but talking a lot in voices lower than usual. They all had so much to say, but the same words kept coming up: "Take me with you." Even our niece, who was on Mao Tse Tung's payroll as a Red Guard, an honor that was reserved only for the most fervent communist regime, begged us in her low voice to take her out of her country and bring her to the United States. Henry's mother didn't ask to go with us. She was happy to die a year later in China, her country, at the age of eighty-four.

The family looked at us as if we had some power to make things better, to get them out of China and away from its miseries. They wanted freedom, and they all had dreams—and the United States held the dreams and hopes of their world. It was a solemn moment when Henry and I finally said good night to them. We felt so powerless and didn't get much sleep that night.

The next morning was time for the good-byes. The day started out misty and foggy. We ate a light breakfast and then waited for our taxi to pick us up. I was a bit anxious. What if the driver was not coming back for us? Finally, by the time the taxi arrived, it was midmorning. The family had given me their information, all the descriptions of their work experience, dates of birth, and resumes, all done in advance.

What a heartbreaking good-bye it was. I am not sure exactly how many, but at least twenty people stood in line; first the friends came forward, then the family, then Henry's mother. Their last good-bye was a hug as they stood by our small eight-passenger taxi. Everyone cried and begged us to stay in touch. I will never forget that moment. I will never forget those good-byes. I felt like such a coward for leaving behind all those faces with all the tears in their eyes. It was one of the most emotional times of the trip.

When we returned home, we tried to bring some of Henry's relatives to the United States, but the red tape made it almost impossible to get anything done. We had to pay for all kinds of research. We finally got one of his deceased brother's sons out of China, but it took us three years.

After a while, the government of China got more flexible. Some of the nephews could start their own businesses in China as long as they invested their own money. We helped another nephew start his furniture business there. After Henry died in 1995, I lost touch with his family, mostly because of the language barrier. I did speak with a niece in California a year later, and she assured me that those in China were doing well. I hope everything is continuing to go well for every one of them.

Chapter 6

Losing our Dream

❦

August 8, 1985, was the beginning of the end of our dream. One of our customers came into the restaurant with another couple just before dinnertime. They asked for drinks at the bar while they waited for a table. The waitress served them a round of drinks, but a few minutes later, she told me that she thought they already had enough and maybe had been drinking at another place. I told her to refuse their requests for more drinks; they got insulted and left. I canceled their food order as they walked out.

I didn't think about it until the man came back around ten that night, sat at the counter and asked the bartender for a drink. My bartenders were all told to cut off anyone whom they thought had had enough to drink. It was not easy for them to do, but it was the law. That night, I had a different person tending the bar. He did not refuse the customer, for he was always worried about some confrontation with any customer. So he served a drink to this already intoxicated man, the same man who had stormed out of the restaurant earlier that evening.

Someone told me, and I ran to the bar to stop the transaction. When I was about halfway to the bar, I met two police officers

71

coming toward the bar. They grabbed the customer and took him out of the building in a rough manner. Their actions took me by surprise. When I asked what happened, no one would tell me anything. I was nervous because it wasn't like the police to treat me like that. We had always been on good terms with all of them. I always prided myself on keeping a good atmosphere in the bar. At the time, on the weekends I had two part-time police women working as waitresses. It took two days before I could find out what had happened.

This customer whom we had refused to serve earlier had gone somewhere else and drank for about four hours. On his way home, the drunk had run over a young man who was in police training and had just put down a road flare on the street after a minor accident. When he was hit, he was severely injured by the drunk, who was driving a Jeep. God only knows how many drinks the man had in the late afternoon before he decided to stop at our restaurant for one more. Apparently, he was so intoxicated that he didn't realize he had run a person over. Our building was large, with four entrances, so I had not seen him come in. It was easy to miss a patron coming or leaving the restaurant.

It didn't take long for the bad publicity to get around the town at full speed. The small local newspaper had some story every day on the front page. No one will ever know how we felt. *Desperate* may be the word I was looking for; I was numb. Henry was so hurt—all this work we had done—and I had to be strong for all of us. During the next few months, sales gradually went down. The town had placed a police car close to our entrance at night to catch anyone who had been drinking too much before coming into our restaurant. We were under surveillance most of the time. Our customers were uncomfortable being the center of attention, so they went elsewhere to eat. Finally, we decided to sell the restaurant. Maybe we could salvage some of our pride and our finances.

Chapter 7

A Desperate Time

※

After this terrible incident, Henry and I didn't know what to do for the first few months. I was hoping to regain some stability and confidence. We were the same people who had always tried to do our best for our customers and employees. Now we were punished for the actions of someone we didn't have control over and made an example for the rest of the bar owners. We became the target of Mothers Against Drunk Driving, or MADD.

Everyone knew that we were desperate. The bills were piling up; customers had turned away from us. I think they were scared to be involved with people who at one time were so well liked and now were on the front page of the local newspaper. They had nothing to do but talk about us.

We kept going for almost a year, and things were getting worse week by week, despite the fact that I also ran a cafeteria at the port in one of the mills. I had taken it over about three years earlier and made it into a thriving business. I was proud of myself, and the small business was growing steadily. It was an easy way to make a few extra dollars. It was a lot of extra work, and I had to be ready to help at any time, but I was able to keep up, going from one business to the other every day. After five months of agony, we knew we had to sell our dream.

We decided to try to find a buyer through word of mouth, but we got just a few offers. So we listed the restaurant with a realtor in February of 1986. We received a couple of offers, but nothing that was acceptable. We kept the restaurant open into the spring of 1986, but we were losing money every day; we were not able to meet the daily expenses. We didn't want to go too deep in the hole. We were already in debt with the suppliers. I was doing the best I could, but we both knew that there wouldn't be anything to salvage if we kept going the way we were. Finally, on May 31, after eight exciting years of hard work and many rewards, we closed the restaurant.

The last night that we were open was the twenty-first birthday of one of our servers, Brenda. Her family had planned a surprise party for her. We had decorated the room in black and white as a joke because she had a white mother and a black father. They were the most beautiful people, and Brenda had become like a daughter to me. I didn't want to tell her that she was having the last celebration at our restaurant, because she was having so much fun with her family and friends. All night, I could not talk much to anyone. I had a big lump in my throat because I knew it was good-bye.

Soon after the restaurant closed, the realtor contacted us. A serious buyer from Seattle, Washington, had made an offer of $650,000 for the restaurant, and we accepted. The down payment had not yet been received, and this concerned us, but we had no choice except to take his offer.

We had to sell both of our houses: the one we had for the cooks to live in while they worked for us at the restaurant, and our family home, which I loved so much. It had a view almost too beautiful to describe. From the same window, we could see both the city and the ocean, yet we were isolated from the noise and traffic of the city. I hated to give it up; I will always remember that home.

Our troubles did not end here. The house we had rented after selling our family home was about to be rented to someone else. We had to move out because our agreement was a two-month lease, which was fine when we agreed to it because we planned to move away to where we had friends as soon as the sale was final. We talked again to the realtor as well as our lawyer and were told that in only a couple of weeks, the sale of the restaurant would be going through. The realtor advised us not to worry, saying that everything would be fine. We could move because all paperwork and money could be sent to our new location. We had made many mistakes taking advice from people who called themselves our friends. In situations like this, as the saying goes, "You really find out who your real friends are." Believe me—those words are so true.

After we sold the house, we were resigned to move somewhere in the United States with nice weather. The Seattle area has rainy weather most of the year. We made our decision to move to Houston, Texas, at the end of June. The day before we left, we had help from lots of friends who loaded the Jartran moving truck. All of us went for pizza, and then we said good-bye. What a sad moment that was.

The next morning we were on our way, leaving all the memories of Port Angeles behind. The trip took us about five days. I was driving the car with Angela and my friend Pat as my companions. Henry and Pat's husband, Dick, were following us in the moving truck, which was filled with all our belongings. Dick helped Henry with the driving. I had sold all the big pieces of furniture before we left. Some never could be replaced, but they were only things. I was left with the best: the love of my husband and daughter. They were the rays of sunshine in my life that kept me going.

That trip to Texas was a real adventure for all of us. I am grateful to Pat and Dick for being with me in those moments. I will always remember their help and miss them forever. In life, you find a few real friends, and real they were.

We arrived in Houston and found an apartment for rent at a good location for work and school. However, we had to wait for our restaurant's final papers to be signed ... and then for the payment that was supposed to be deposited into our bank any day. By then, we were running out of money, and I was scared. It turned out that this move was a bad one. Wages were low, and the oil business, Texas's main industry, was declining. The first job that Henry got was working in a deli, where he was paid $6.50 an hour. The first week he worked only thirty hours. When he got home with his first paycheck, he sat at the kitchen table and cried like a baby. It was a sad day for the three of us. We had moved to Houston just when the economy was at its worst. There were closing signs everywhere, the housing market was at the low point, and empty buildings stood all over town. The oil drilling industry was closing, and jobs were scarce.

I found a job at a new Target that was about to open. The work was hard, and the management was rude to the employees. Every day after work, I cried on my way home. I stayed at Target for a couple of weeks and then found a job managing a cafeteria for an oil company. It was much better. It didn't pay much, but the owners were fair. I made money for them, so after a month, they gave me a raise of twenty dollars a week, making my earnings a grand total of two hundred dollars a week. Henry got another job working in a Chinese restaurant. He worked twelve hours a day, six days a week, and sometimes they called him in on his day off. We barely survived. His asthma was acting up, probably because of the stress.

By the end of July, we still had not received the money for the sale of the restaurant, so we contacted the realtor again. He assured us that the money would arrive soon. The money would be enough to pay our bills, and with the small amount left over, we could start a small business again. We waited and called and waited some more, and finally the realtor called to tell us that the buyer had decided to back out of the deal. By then we were desperate. We begged the realtor to find another buyer for our business, but to no avail.

I am not sure, but I believe that the realtor had something to do with the buyer's decision. By then, we were too far in debt to get a new business started. It was costing us too much to travel, and the bills were getting higher. The payment to the bank on the restaurant was six months behind. We received the bad news that we still could not sell the restaurant, and the bank took over the property. They had been patient, but it had been over nine months and we didn't have any recourse. We had to let it go down with the ship.

In addition to this disappointment, the trial for the man who had caused us all this mess had been delayed. The lawyers were gathering evidence while everyone waited for the recovery of the young man who had been hit by the drunk driver. We kept in touch with the lawyer who was preparing the case against him. I wanted to get that mess finished, but they dragged the case on for over four years. We were in limbo—always worried about what they could do to us.

We had no friends in Houston, and with Henry's asthma, he was always having difficulty breathing. The weather in Texas was not good for him, and our daughter Angela was showing signs of respiratory problems as well. It was a sad time for me, but I had to keep going for my family. We had nothing left, so once again we moved, this time to Montreal, to be closer to my family. We packed and left Houston on a Sunday in late summer and moved to a tiny basement apartment, so I unpacked only what we really needed. The rest stayed in boxes stacked in an area of the living room.

Henry and I both got jobs in different restaurants. Like two slaves, we worked day and night. Thank God Angela was such a good girl; she kept us going. I had been a smiling person all my life, but now I wore a mask. I could not smile anymore. I was in constant anguish. I could not get back to normal, and I always had to fake my feelings, because I was the only moral support for my husband and daughter.

Angela had to attend a French immersion school in Montreal, which was difficult for her because she did not speak French. At this time she was fifteen years old, which made her situation ever harder. She missed her friends. I saw her sad face, but I couldn't do much about it. It was difficult for me not to be able to comfort her.

Work in Montreal was not easy to find. After a while, I found a diner to lease on Saint Jacques Street. The rent was low enough, so we decided that we could make a living there. The diner was open from 7:00 a.m. to 6:00 p.m. Monday through Saturday and closed on Sunday. We were open for breakfast, lunch, and part of the late afternoon. This work went considerably well until we had a robbery. When we opened one morning, we found that the place had been ransacked. Everything was on the floor. What a mess! The feeling of insecurity that came with the robbery made us very uncomfortable.

A month later, Henry had trouble with his leg and had to have a vein removed. He was in the hospital for a few days. It was a bit hard for me, and Henry was worried about my being alone in the diner at closing. When the lease ended, we decided not to renew it, and once again, Henry and I had to make a decision to move. This move took us to Lawrence, Massachusetts. We arrived June 26, 1987.

Henry got a job right away at a Chinese restaurant in Portsmouth, New Hampshire, where he also had to live during the week. It was about an hour away from Lawrence. I had driven to my sister Louiselle's in Methuen, Massachusetts, a week earlier to rent a place in the area that we could move into right away. However, the day before we were to leave Montreal, I received a call from the landlord, saying that he had decided not to rent the apartment. My furniture was already packed in the truck. I was not too worried because I could look for another place when I got to Methuen.

The next morning, my brother-in-law who was going to drive the truck for me told me that he could not do it because of some emergency. Now I was in real trouble. I had to drive my car and I had no driver for the truck. I got on the phone, and after a few hours, I found someone from U-Haul who was willing to drive the truck.

Angela and I left early the next morning, and the entire trip went well. We drove eight and a half hours without any incidents. Even at the American border, the agents were helpful. I dropped off the trailer and car at Louiselle's home. The next morning, I started driving around the streets of Methuen and Lawrence with Angela, looking for a place to rent. Since Henry was working, I was on my own to find a place to lease. The search was harder than I had anticipated, but I finally found a place after three days of looking.

As I was talking to the landlord, I noticed a sad look on Angela's face. I took her aside and asked what was bothering her. With tears in her eyes, she said, "But Mom, the carpet is orange." I reassured her that I would cover the carpet with rugs and it would be fine. I will never forget her look. She had no choice but to follow Henry and me wherever we went. She had been used to a good life, but now everything had changed.

The lawsuit was still pending, and I was walking on eggshells. I found out that both lawyers were gathering evidence around the small town of Port Angeles. Half of the people had been questioned for one reason or another. I am not sure what they expected to find at that time. I became so depressed that I didn't want to go on. I was told that the trial would be moved two hundred miles, from Port Angeles to Seattle, Washington, because everyone knew us in the small town. The judge excused himself because he was our friend.

The lawyer had rented a large room at the Sheraton Hotel in Seattle just to store all the depositions and other papers—and one room for me since he wanted me in the courtroom every day during the trial. The case was supposed to take at least a month, and we were anxious to have peace of mind.

Henry and I were both working but could not get out of the hole. Living expenses took every cent from month to month. I was tired of all those moves, and I wanted this move to Lawrence to be the last move I would ever have to make. I was at a point in my life where I desperately needed stability, friends, and familiarity. I had reached my limit. I told Henry that I wanted to stay close to my sister in Methuen. He insisted that we move closer to his work. We had discussed this before moving to Lawrence. He thought that I should stay close to the city of Boston, perhaps somewhere in a suburb so we could be close to everything and not have to move again. Angela was getting older and probably would get married the not-too-distant future. I wanted to stay close to her since she had been our only source of joy for a long time, and I would not jeopardize this relationship for anything in the world. I felt that I deserved that after all the compromises I had made in my life. I did not want to be more than ten miles from the rest of my family so we could be close enough to visit anytime we wanted without having to take a day off to travel. Henry finally agreed that we would make our home in Lawrence.

By the end of the summer, Angela enrolled as a junior at Lawrence High School and was so happy that she did not lose a year by transferring from the school in Canada. However, we had to talk to the principal to persuade him to let her start in that class. On our way out of the principal's office that day, Angela yelled, "Yeah!"

I said, "Angela, be quiet, or he will change his mind." But I will always remember what he did for my daughter; this school gave her a chance to be herself again. She made good friends, and life was almost normal once more.

I had been a server at a Denny's restaurant in Salem, New Hampshire, for three months when the district manager asked me to take over the management. I wasn't interested, but other jobs were not easy to find and management paid better wages, so I accepted. I had three months of training to learn their standards. The work was hard. Denny's was open 24/7 and I was doing many night shifts. On weekends I worked twelve-hour shifts, from 5:00 p.m. to 5:00 a.m. The clientele wasn't first class, with lots of drunks for customers, especially during the weekend nights. I was supposed to have an assistant, but most of the time I was acting as a manager and a bouncer. At five feet tall, I was supposed to keep the place safe for the other patrons! I was lucky that the police department liked me; they always watched out for me, driving by and taking turns for their coffee breaks. I felt safe and thankful for their support and watchful eyes.

On a Friday afternoon in October 1988, before the start of the trial against the drunk driver who had been the cause of the loss of our restaurant business in Port Angeles, my lawyer called and said that the case had been settled out of court. What a relief it was. I would have had to stay in Seattle during the trial, and we didn't know how long it would have taken. My lawyer had said that it would probably be lengthy because of all the depositions he had taken. I was happy because finally we wouldn't have this burden on our minds all the time, and I would not have to be away from Angela, who was now seventeen. We had insurance, but since it had taken four and a half years for the case to get to court, we had lost everything. It was one of the most publicized cases because the organization MADD had just started, and everyone wanted a piece of the action. The ordeal had nearly destroyed us, broken us to pieces. Finally, there was some peace in our lives for a while.

Those four-plus years of waiting had taken a toll on Henry's health. He was getting more asthma attacks and most of the time was in a sad mood. He was not the happy person that he used to be. At that point, Henry and I both worked six days a week. I tried to pay some of the bills that we had left behind, but it was too hard for me. We couldn't get ahead very fast, but we had each other, even though we were apart most of the week.

I had promised myself that Angela would have a college education no matter what happened. She would get the education that I had missed. We would send her to a state college that was less expensive and had a good reputation. I had saved a few dollars, and she received a scholarship from her high school. The first two years of college weren't too bad, but the last two were harder. It took everything we had to make ends meet, but that was okay. It was no sacrifice since she made us very proud .She was always doing well; she was a very hard worker and still is. She is a perfectionist. Everything has to be done to the best she can achieve. We were happy our daughter was going to college. At least one of our dreams was coming true.

When she started college, I missed her so much because it was the first time we had been apart. Three weeks after she started, I went to the college to visit her and bring her some paper as an excuse to see her. She looked happy and was all business, as always. She took school very seriously, and it was a bit of a relief to see her sure of herself and enjoying freedom for the first time.

We were proud of how well she was doing; she was the president of her class. She graduated in 1993. I was the proudest mother in the world, and Henry was the proudest father. She took a month off to relax, and in July she worked part time for her cousin at a sidewalk café at nearby Hampton Beach. She lived at home to economize because the money wasn't too good, but it was a good experience.

I was alone a lot of the time that we lived in Lawrence. Henry came home from Portsmouth only on Sundays for eight years until he got sick. I was working full time, but I needed more than that. I didn't have any friends, just coworkers—no one close enough to confide in. As their boss, I could not get close to any of them. Moreover, the number of hours I worked left no time for enjoyment. When Henry came on the weekend, he was tired from six days of long hours at work. I tried to make our lives as pleasant as possible. I don't know why he didn't try to get a job closer to home to be with us more often. I asked him many times, but he refused to look for any other job. I didn't feel loved anymore. It was not a good time for me. Angela was getting older and soon out of college. She had her own friends, her work, and her studies. I was tired and lonely and just wanted roots for my family and me.

In addition to Denny's, I worked part time during the day doing real estate, insurance, and a few other jobs so time for sleep was at a minimum. The loneliness and pressure of my job was a bit much for me as well as hard on my health. I started to feel sick. I had memory lapses that scared me, but with insurance only for major catastrophes, I hesitated to see a doctor. Finally, I had to make a decision and I went to see one at the hospital in Lowell. I was diagnosed with exhaustion and put on medication for rest. A nurse called me twice a day for over a month. It took me a while, but I got better, although it took me about a year to finally be myself again.

It was another scary thing I had been through. I never told anyone about it. I didn't want to burden anyone with my problems.

Chapter 8

Finding Martine

❦

All those years, I had been looking for my other daughter. I had tried many ways, without success. I wanted to find her so maybe I could have some kind of relationship with her before she might get married. August 1994, Henry was on vacation and had a routine physical done one morning. After lunch, we went for a car ride, and when we returned home, there was a call from his doctor, who wanted Henry to return right away to the office. When we arrived, the doctor told us that one of Henry's lungs didn't look normal and he wanted more tests done. The results showed cancer.

We had finally come out of our financial mess. I didn't want to believe that Henry had cancer and needed an operation as soon as possible. On October 4, he had a lung removed. I stayed in the hospital all day. When the operation was over, the doctor told me that everything had gone well, so I went home.

I had some rest, and the next morning after I called the hospital, I was sitting at the dining room table having coffee before leaving to visit Henry when the phone rang. The man on the phone asked, "Are you alone?"

"Yes", I answered.

He then told me to sit down, that he had something very important to tell me. By then I was shaking because I thought the news was about Henry. Then he said, "We have found your daughter."

Those words I had dreamed of hearing shocked me. The feeling was indescribable. Should I be happy, scared, or was it a bad joke? I made him repeat the words he had just said. Yes, I had heard right; they had found my daughter. For a few seconds I could not talk. Then I asked the man some questions.

One of them was, "Is she well?"

Then I asked, "Does she have children?"

For some crazy reason, I hoped to find that she was single so I could treat her like a little girl for a while. The man told me that he had had a conversation with her over the phone. He told me that she was married and had children—he'd heard a baby making noise while they were talking. She was in good health and lived near Montreal.

I asked him, "Does she want to see me?"

He said, "For now, you and she will have to take your time to get used to the idea of being found." He added, "You cannot make contact with her until she is ready. You can write to her only through my office."

That first letter was so hard to write. Would I be able to say the right words? Should I tell her everything? I had made a mistake once, and it had caused me to lose her. I could not make that mistake again. I was very happy but scared at the same time. What if she didn't want to see me after all these years? I had imagined taking her in my arms and holding her tight so that she would not get away again.

I had waited so long; I could wait a little longer. Besides, I had my husband to care for. I wanted to share the news with him, but it was no time for a surprise. He had been in intensive care all night and was far from cured from the lung cancer. I was so scared of losing him that I could not be as happy as I wanted to be after finding my daughter. The emotions that I experienced that day can't be described. I started to feel sick. The day that I had dreamed about all my life was here, but I could not enjoy it as I had hoped. I was scared to laugh or be excited, feeling all that joy and sadness all at once. I had no one to share my feelings with, mostly because I had never told anyone about Martine, except my daughter, Angela, my husband, Henry, and my sister Gisele.

A few days later, I told Angela that I had found her sister. She reacted with enthusiasm, but I knew she was also worried about a new sister. Would there be a big change in her life? She had been the only child in our house for twenty-three years, and as a family, we were very close. Now she would have to share with someone she did not know. She had many questions. It wasn't only me I had to think about. I didn't want to hurt the two people that I loved so much.

Henry got out of the hospital a week later. I wanted to tell him, but I was scared of his reaction. He had been in agreement with me that I should try to find Martine, but now he wasn't well. I didn't want to upset him, but I had to tell him. There wasn't any way around it; he had to know. I don't remember how I told him, but as always, he was happy for me and asked just a few questions. He was staying alone at home while I was working at the mall in Salem, New Hampshire. I worried about him, but I had to work because I was the only source of income. I would call him as often as I could to check on him. He never complained and slowly got better.

By late November, Henry was out of bed and back in the kitchen in our house, cooking for Angela and me. He was such a good cook; he could make anything taste good. I never saw anyone cook the way he did. By Christmas, he was much better and insisted on having a party. I helped him with the cooking, as he tired easily. We had friends and family over for dinner. He truly enjoyed himself.

Henry had always liked to have people around him but didn't have many friends because of his work. He had always been in the kitchen in each of the places where he worked, and after long hours, he would come home right away. He liked sports of any kind. He could tell you the name of any player, his position, and how much he was paid. Everyone used to ask him questions just to see if he would know the answer. He never missed one that I can remember. He had a wonderful memory. He had even known the names of all the customers in our restaurant. He was remarkable. Although his health wasn't good now, he was walking every day to get stronger. He was hoping to get back to work full time. I kept watching him doing the best he could to get back to normal, but it wasn't working.

At the end of November 1994, I received my first letter from Martine. So many emotions went through me. Sitting at the dining room table, Angela, Henry, and I read the letter. We studied all her words and hoped to meet her soon. I answered that letter through the agent. Before Christmas, I got another letter with some pictures of her. We must have looked at those pictures a million times, trying to discover a resemblance. We agreed that she looked like me.

From that day on I wrote to her often, but I was very careful not to scare her. I tried to make sure that I let her know that she had a family that would be very happy to have her sharing our joy. I told her that she had a sister, and a step-father who would be happy to have another daughter to love.

On February 19, 1995, Martine called me for the first time. It was my birthday. I was in my bedroom sitting on the floor. She had such a soft voice. She told me that they had just come home from skiing with the children— her daughter who was four, and her son who was two. She told me many things that I can't remember, for the call was such a surprise. What a gift for my birthday! I got up, went into the living room, and tried to tell Angela and Henry what Martine had told me. I was so excited that I repeated the same things over and over.

In March, we talked again and she invited me to her town to meet her. As I was the only manager in the mall pretzel eatery where I worked, I would have to ask the big boss to replace me for a few days. No need to say that I got organized quickly. Two weeks later she was able to replace me for a few days, and by April, we were able to go to meet Martine. She had made reservations at the hotel for us since I wasn't familiar with the town. On the way, I bought a bouquet of flowers for her. We arrived at the hotel at noon, and when I went into the room, I saw a bouquet of flowers on the table by the window. Extraordinarily, it was the same kind of bouquet as the one I had in my hand. It was almost scary.

I called to say that we had arrived, and we scheduled a time for her to come to the hotel to meet us. When she knocked at the door that afternoon, it was the most indescribable moment, not only for me but all of us. When I took her in my arms and hugged her, I felt our hearts pounding hard. I introduced her to Henry and Angela. After a few words, Angela and Henry left us alone to talk for a while.

It was such an emotional conversation. None of the things I had wanted to tell her during those past years seemed important anymore. I just wanted to look at her. She was sitting there, my daughter, looking so small. I studied all her movements in those moments. It felt like a dream. We made a date for dinner that evening so I could meet her husband. We had an unforgettable evening and took pictures. We promised to visit again soon. She left with her husband around 11:00 p.m. The emotions of that day had me so excited that I could not sleep all night. Reality really set in the next morning before we left for home. I was able to hold and touch her! After Henry, Angela, and I got home, we called Martine often, and she called us. We invited them to visit us during the summer vacation.

Soon after this joyful reunion, Henry learned that he had prostate cancer and had to have another operation or take a chance that it might not be dangerous for a while. He just wanted to get well and not have to go back to the hospital. He wanted to be finished with pills and doctors, but instead of getting well the cancer spread. He chose the operation, but it was a mistake because he had pain for a long time and never felt good after that. He wanted to go back to work; that was all he was hoping for.

In July 1995, we had a party for Martine to celebrate the first time that she was coming home. We had invited all our good friends to welcome her. We had a wonderful time. A day or two after everyone left, I noticed that Henry seemed to be dizzy. When I asked he told me that it had been going on for a while. I made an appointment with his doctor, who told us that nothing was wrong. I had an argument with him and told him that I knew my husband and to look again until he found the problem. I was right. The doctor found that the cancer had spread to the pituitary gland and was close to his brain. He started chemotherapy immediately. I took him to the hospital almost every day for his treatment, but I didn't see any improvement; he was getting weaker.

Henry liked to do grocery shopping, so that became his outing. And it was good for me to know he was going out. But by October, he didn't want to go out much and was in and out of the hospital—the last time was at the end of November. The night before, after I came home from work, I helped him put on his socks and discovered that his feet and part of his legs were blue, as if he had been badly beaten.

The next morning, I took him to the hospital again. I didn't know that this would be the last time. Angela and I visited him late one night. Angela had a good talk with her father, and I sat there and listened to Henry giving her advice. It was very touching. The next morning when I visited, I realized that he was very sick. Just looking at him made me feel guilty for being so helpless, at a time when he needed me so much. I had always been the one who was able to fix everything. I was Super Mom and Super Wife because I wanted to be. And most of the time, I was able to produce small miracles. I had always found a way to get things done one way or another, and at times I think I enjoyed the chaos and turbulence of my life. However, with Henry's illness, it was a daily challenge for me to continue as the miracle worker. It just became routine to do what I was asked to do or where I was to be.

I fed Henry a few spoonfuls of soup that he usually liked, but he wanted to go back to sleep. I went home to get some rest, but as soon as I got there, I got a call from the hospital to go back because they thought Henry didn't have long to live. I called Angela at work, and she barely made it in time to see her father go. During that time, I became frantic, running in the corridor, begging the nurse to do something. He couldn't die; I did not want him to leave us. He was gone in no time. I had hoped he would get better. We had gone through so much together—we could do that again.

Henry was buried on December 7, 1995, a cold day with snow falling. I had lost my best friend. It was the saddest day of my life, but as always, I didn't show much of my sorrow. I buried myself in my work. I still had Angela and Martine, and my two grandchildren. This did help.

When Henry got sick, Angela worked days, and we both took turns checking on him. It took me a long time to get used to the idea that he was gone forever. I still miss him, and I probably always will.

Our insurance did not cover all the services that Henry required. After he was gone, I was left with $74,000 in hospital bills. He had a life insurance policy and after some negotiation with the hospital, I ended up with a few dollars left, which I invested in a down payment on a condominium. I finally made it through the first year, and then I slowly got used to being alone. It didn't scare me as much anymore. When someone tells you that with time you get used to almost anything, do believe it.

However, I was lonely, with no one to talk to. And because it was painful for Angela too, I avoided the subject with her. Then I became good friends with Jackie, who had lost her husband one year earlier, and we consoled each other. For the first two years after Henry died, I was working as hard as I could so I wouldn't have to be alone, especially at home.

My reunion with Martine and her family in April 1995 and Henry's death in December 1995 were extremely emotional times for me. Although Henry had cancer and was in and out of the hospital at the time all this happened, I am sure he was happy for me. He was able to visit Martine and her children, Laurence and Charles Antoine, in Quebec, and they came to visit us once before he died. Henry loved the grandchildren, and they loved him. All his friends had children, and they were always playing with him. He was as much a kid as they were. I wish he could have seen Angela's two sons before he died. I just hope he can see them from above.

In 1998, Angela met Eric Heenan and for the first time she became serious about a young man. I was happy and a bit worried at the same time. I wanted her to be happy, but marriage would take away my little girl. I knew that I would miss her terribly. I had lost everything—she was the last of my treasures—but I had to let her go in order to keep her. In a way, their relationship was a dream come true. It was important for me to make sure that when my time came to leave this world, Angela would have someone to love and protect her.

On December 31, 2000, Angela and Eric were married. She was

the most beautiful bride in the world, and Eric was so handsome in his tuxedo. With tears in my eyes, I heard them say, "I do", and then everything was a blur for a few minutes. The only one missing was Henry. How proud he would have been. I am sure that from above he was watching out for his little girl. Eric is the best father and husband. I couldn't be happier to have him as my son-in-law. Angela and Eric are doing well in their life.

Martine and Robert are also doing well. I do not get to see them very often because of the traveling distance. However, we do the best we can to stay close. Her children are now older, and life goes on.

Chapter 9

New Beginnings

I still had hopes of getting back into my own business someday, but with time, the idea became less and less attractive to me. After Henry's death, I continued to work even harder. I had a good job, and I dedicated most of my time competing with the bigger franchises of the pretzel company. I was doing well at work for the size of my store; I had the top sales of the year. I liked the fact that I was my own boss. I was working for an absentee owner. I had to make all the decisions since most of the time the owner was out of the area. It was a demanding job, long hours, no weekends off, but at that point, I was alone at home most of the time. Henry was gone, Angela had her own life, and my friend Jacky spent a lot of time in Florida. The few other friends I had were couples. It was always uncomfortable for me to go out with them. I ached with loneliness.

I was looking for something, but I was not sure what I wanted. Maybe it was reconnection. I wanted some type of accomplishment, maybe taking something and molding it to a new shape to make something extraordinary. I was just a dreamer, and I did not think I would be able to make my dream come true. But maybe I could prove myself wrong. Everything I had learned up to that point had been from reading or doing. I had never been afraid of new challenges. They were adventures to me, and I loved that.

At sixty-three I had been a widow for over six years, and my friends wanted me to find a new husband. They were all working on it. I was introduced to every one of their male friends, but I was not interested. Their tastes in men were much different from mine. I met men who were short, tall, rich, and poor—you name it. I was getting fed up of being put on the market without my approval. I wanted to meet a man on my own who met more of my expectations so I would have an excuse to refuse those surprise encounters.

To meet someone about my age was not easy. At the beginning, it was a real chore just to meet someone new. Most of the men I met were so different from those I used to know. Many were divorced or never married, had a family, or had lots of baggage. It took me a long time to find someone who would share my values.

I became disillusioned and decided to give up the idea of finding the right man. By then, I was used to being alone and independent. As always, if I wanted something, I had to get it myself, so I did. Finally, I decided to go shopping and buy what I wanted. I found a place called The Right One, and it cost me two thousand dollars to get on the shopping list. For that kind of money, I could have the prospect investigated, interrogated, and photographed. This was a precaution I wanted to take. I am a family-oriented person. I had a good family to protect, and I wasn't going to take a chance on hurting them. Still, I met many losers through The Right One.

One was a handsome, well-dressed man. We met for dinner, and first we had a glass of wine. At that time, I was a social smoker, so I took out my cigarettes, and he said, "Oh, you smoke. I left mine in the car. I'll go get them. I like to smoke too."

You are already trying to deceive me, I thought.

Later, during the dinner, he said to me, "I have a beautiful hot tub, and I would like you to try it with me."

I answered, "It sounds good, but I can't make it tonight. I will go to your house tomorrow afternoon."

He was happy with my answer and called the next morning to say that he was anxious to see me, and that he had lots of champagne on ice. When I didn't show up, he called for two days, but I didn't answer the phone. I was very impressed by his relentless manner. By then, his interest must have faded because I did not hear from him again!

I received another call from The Right One. This time a man asked me to meet him for coffee. I wasn't too enthusiastic about doing this again, but my sister Louiselle convinced me to give it a try. I was all dressed to go, and then I changed my mind.

Louiselle said to me, "Just go take a look, and if you don't like what you see, pretend that you have to go to the bathroom and then leave by the back door." It sounded like a good idea to me. We had a good laugh about it later.

I met James at Applebee's in Londonderry, New Hampshire. I am not going to say that it was love at first sight, but we had a pleasant conversation and made a date for a movie for the next weekend. A year later, on July 26, 2005, Jim and I were married.

Jim and I are very happy; we share most of the same values. Family is important to both of us. We each have two children, and they have melded into a single family. Our children are becoming more like brothers and sisters. It is such a nice feeling to see everyone happily discussing work, family, or any subject. Each one has views of their own, and they don't always agree, but this is why I love them the way they are.

After I married Jim, new grandchildren were added to my family. It is so nice to have our children and grandchildren together as often as we can. I am no longer alone, and I love it! Jim and I are extremely lucky. Our lives are filled with family and love. We have been blessed!

I have moved around the United States and Canada for many years; now that I am retired, I live closer to most of my family, and although we don't always visit as much as I would like, it is a wonderful feeling to know that they are close to me. Finally, I have a normal life. I now enjoy every minute of my life, every day. I try to stay away from dilemmas. There are always tribulations, but peace is what I cherish most at this time in my life.

For the first time in my life, I am free to do what I like. I always wanted to go back to school. I have always had a need to learn—I was never satisfied—but something always kept me from pursuing that dream. I wanted to write a book someday, but I asked myself, *how can I be a writer?* I never thought I would write a book about myself. I did the things that other people do—I got a house, a business, and two daughters—but there was always a void. I was never satisfied with what I had achieved.

To begin filling that void, I enrolled in a writing class in September 2006. I met a group of interesting women about my age and with the same interests. I have always liked to write. I could say anything I wanted without any argument or contradiction. I do believe that writing has helped me over the years. I confided with paper and a pen in my hand. I was sharing my worries and my joy with someone who would listen to me without making judgment.

I always admired my mother's talent for art and writing and had tried as a little girl to recreate some of her drawings, but to no avail. My eyes and my hands did not work together. When I retired, I began taking drawing lessons, something I had wanted to do for a long time. It turns out that I am not so bad after all. It makes me happy to discover that I have some of my mother's talent. And to top off my new adventures, I started piano lessons. I enjoy all three activities, and I have met many interesting people. If I had the time

I would take more classes, but there are only so many hours in a day. If my health continues to be good, I will be able to learn other things. I am involved in many social activities. Having worked all my life with the public, these activities are irresistible for me.

A few years ago, I returned for a reunion in the small town of Saint-Eusèbe, where I grew up. No one had changed much; most of the people had remained in the same area. A great adventure was not a big part of their lives. I was disappointed but not surprised. Everyone was happy and having a good time, and so was I. It was emotional and thrilling at the same time to see my classmates and old friends, even two of my old boyfriends whom I didn't even recognize. It made me realize how much my taste had changed over the years.

I visited the home where I was raised. It looked about the same but older. Only the house was still standing. The grange and the stable were gone, destroyed by time and lack of attention. The house was mostly hidden by large trees that grew where once there was a large field. The three small bushes on the side of the house were now huge trees. The driveway had almost disappeared under those trees. This reunion with my past was a reminder of many good times and bad times, and it showed me how much my life had changed since those days.

I could feel the loneliness of those long-ago years and the uncertainty of those moments. I could see myself playing ball with my sister in the driveway ... the apple trees that I liked to sit under and read. It was such a quiet and calm place to be on a summer afternoon. I remembered one specific day under that tree when I was older. I had tried to learn how to play the accordion there, but after trying to make some music for a while, my sister asked me to give it up. There was no hope for me to make it in the music world! It was the end of my music career. The long road where we could see for a long distance was still there. When we were young, we used to watch our father coming home from the village on that road. All our hideouts, our refuges, had now disappeared.

It still is a lonely place with only memories, some good, some not so good. Someone else lives there now, they say, to get away from the noise of the city. I am sure the new owner's wish has exceeded his expectations.

Chapter 10

Stages of Life

৽

There are many stages in one's life, the first one being the early years of childhood and school. For me, school was my first experience with strangers, and I had difficult times. I was smaller than the other children. My height made me feel different, but it made me more competitive, and the results were always better than the expectations needed to work harder. The results were my reward. I will always remember my first teacher, Miss Janette, and the lasting effect she had on me. She taught me self-esteem and confidence.

I have realized that some of the examples I saw many times in my early years served me later in life—not that they stopped me from making my own mistakes, but sometimes they caused me to think more clearly.

The next stage begins with work. My first jobs gave me feelings of responsibility and independence. It was scary to have to be responsible for my own destiny. It was also very exciting to be on my own and experience everything in this new world of work. The loneliness and separation from my family was hard for me. As with most young people my age, I missed the trust and love of home. I was scared to take risks, but the fears passed. I became adventurous.

And then there is the third stage of falling in love, getting married, having children, and keeping up with the Joneses. These were important times. We don't realize how fast these stages go by. It is like a train ride. We see everything out the window, and we don't have the time to take a second look. The train speeds along, and it will stop only when it gets to its next destination, where suddenly it will stop and let us out. With all our baggage, we stand on the platform somewhat disoriented. We are still uncertain about why we are here. There will always be questions about the future. That stage is still a mystery.

Once these stages have passed by, the wheels of life start all over. My children married, and now I have grandchildren. It is time for me to enjoy life all over again. I have more time to do the things I enjoy. I can take time to smell the roses, as they say.

Rose Aimee means "roses are love." At last, my name and my life fit together. At this stage in my life, I try to take the time to experience the feelings that surround me. Again, I find more joy in the simple things than I ever did before. I will not relax until I have done it all!

Chapter 11

Grandchildren

I now have four grandchildren. Martine's daughter Laurence was born in Montreal. She has grown into a beautiful and smart young woman. So far, she is the only granddaughter. When she was four years old, I gave her a white summer dress covered with pink flowers. She did not want to wear anything else for a week. Her mother had to wash it at night when she was sleeping.

Her son, Charles-Antoine, was also born in Montreal. He is becoming a wonderful young man. When I look at him, I remember when he was two years old and such a little man, charming and so cute and loveable, and he still is to this day. We used to go to Cape Cod for a week of vacation. One night I was babysitting for Martine, and when I put him to bed, he kept coming downstairs to ask for something. It was an excuse not to go to bed. The fourth or sixth time he came to the top of the stairs to ask for something I told him in a loud voice, "Go to sleep!"

He ran back to bed and then came back right away and asked one more question. He said, "Grandma, when you talk loud, does it mean that you are mad at me?"

It took me by surprise. I am not sure what I told him, but I reassured him that I wasn't mad at him and said that he had to go to sleep if he wanted to go to the beach the next day. In the middle of the night, he found his way to my bed. He felt safe with me. I didn't get much sleep, but my grandson was happy. I love him so much, and I miss him, especially those days when he was a toddler. He told me about everything. He loved to talk, and I will never forget those tête-à-têtes. Those were moments I will cherish for the rest of my life. I count myself very lucky to have Laurence and Charles-Antoine and wish I had more time with them, but I know that I might never have had the chance to know them at all, so thank you, God.

My grandson William Henry Heenan is Angela and Eric's older son, my pride and joy. He is a little gentleman. His dark hair is always well combed, and he is good-looking too. I enjoy his company, and since I spent lots of time with him, there is no need to say that I am attached to him. He was the first grandchild whose early childhood I could share.

My fourth grandchild, Andrew Yee Heenan, is the youngest grandchild. He is the most lovable child I know. He is the friendly one, happy and smiling all the time. He is smart and never forgets anything. He is my little angel, and I love him more every day, if that is possible.

My stepdaughter, Diane, has two sons, Tyler and Devon. They are the heroes of William and Andrew, whose admiration for their teenage cousins is without limit. My husband's son, Jim Jr., and his family live in California.

I am very blessed with my family. There is nothing better than those Saturday night family dinners. Food is the best way to get everyone together. I do love to make a good meal. Everyone talks at the same time, and I sit there listening to all the happy noise and enjoy every minute. As I said, I am thankful for these blessings.

Christmas is the best time we all share. Everyone enjoys

watching the little ones' faces light up as they admire the tree, the decorations, and the gifts that Santa brings to them. What a glorious moment it is.

I would not give up what I have accomplished for anything in the world. I have been hoping for this reward my entire life ... and here I have it all.

Chapter 12

Final Thoughts

❦

One sunny day when I was in my early twenties, I was walking on the sidewalk and saw my shadow. I noted that my head was turned downward, and I saw the posture of my body. That shadow made me realize that I had to get away from this environment, so in a matter of a few days, I had made my decision to move to a big city. I am not sure if it was a good decision, but it was my beginning.

When I look back at my life, I think that I was a wanderer looking to find the right path but going through some of the swamps of life at the same time. When I was on flat land, I enjoyed every step, but my character was not satisfied until I tried a new path. Unconsciously, I would wander away from the easy path again and again. Each time, the wandering left me with a lesson that I learned but could not teach. They say that you learn from your mistakes. Well, I learned a great deal.

Each challenge for my siblings and me was only another moment in our lives, and we accommodated ourselves to them. The time we spent together growing up wasn't the best, but we had each other. There wasn't any rivalry between us; we were too busy trying to survive and counting the days until the time we could be on our own and try to get a better life. We had no jealousy. We were all in the same boat, and no one knew how to swim. One by one, we used a raft to get to the shore that was the closest, and every one of us made it one way or the other. My siblings and I all landed on a different island, and each of us made the best of our situation.

I think of my life as an adventure, and the survival skills that I learned as a child—not to panic or give up—helped me later in life. When I look back, I probably would start all over again. Defeats and triumphs have taught me how to survive. That is how I feel today. I am happy with what I have. When I look at my surroundings and see all that I have to be thankful for, that is the best victory I could ever achieve. Good family, good friends, nice home, no hunger or cold—these are what I call the victories of a lifetime. I have fought for and won all of them.